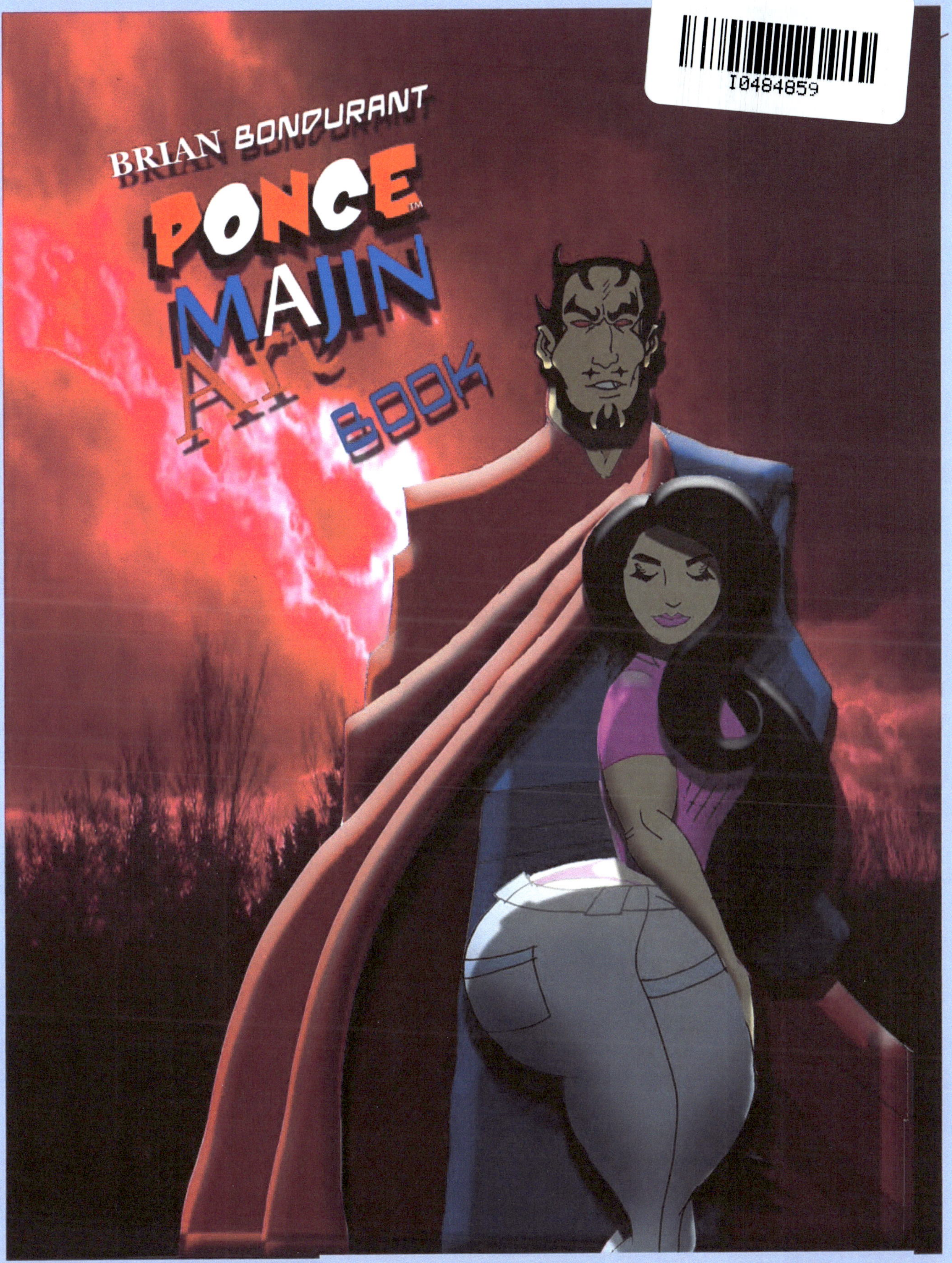

BRIAN BONDURANT
PONCE™
MAJIN
ART
BOOK

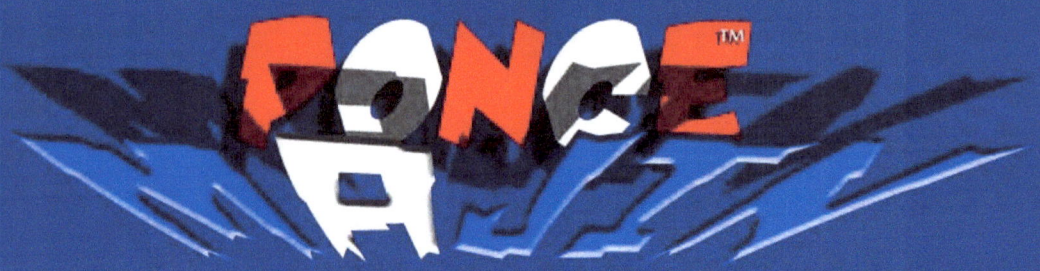

Episodes: 1 - 3

"HATERS BE HATIN'!"

WHO THE HELL DOES THIS GUY THINK HE IS COMING TO MY COUNTRY AND TAKING AWAY ONE OF MY WOMEN?! WELL, SHE'S NOT MY WOMAN! BUT, YOU KNOW WHAT I MEAN! FANCY BASTARD *VANDALO OPRESO* FROM BELLEZA REINO!!! IF YOU WAS THE SHYT OVER THERE, WHY THE HELL DID YOU COME TO PONCE?! I WAS TRYIN' TO HIT THAT! COUNT DRACULA LOOKIN' BASTARD!

A LOT OF THINGS DON'T ADD-UP WITH THAT GUY. SO, I'D HAVE TO AGREE WITH YOU, THERE. HE IS A BIT TOO MUCH ABRA-CADABRA, INN'T HE?

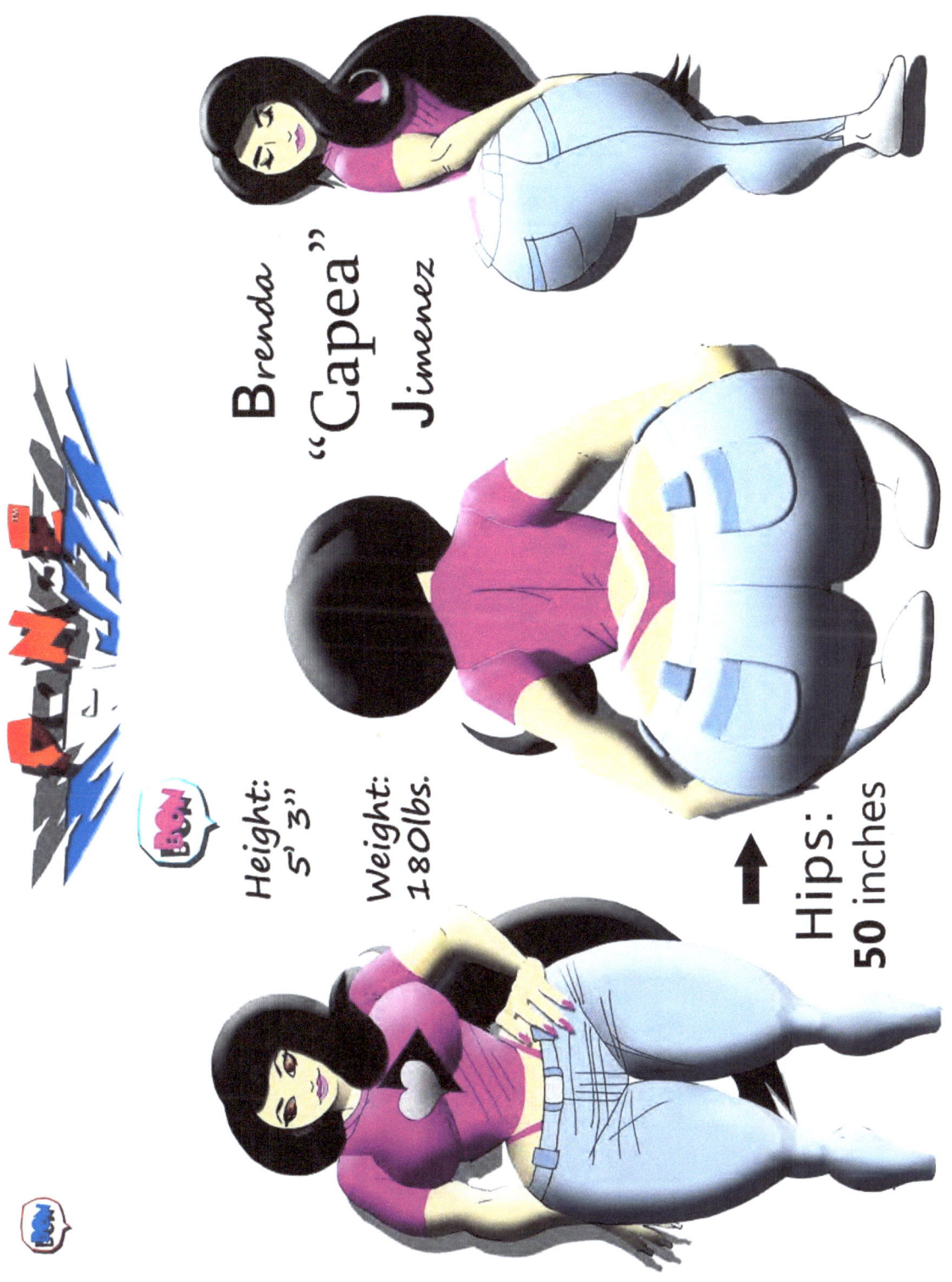

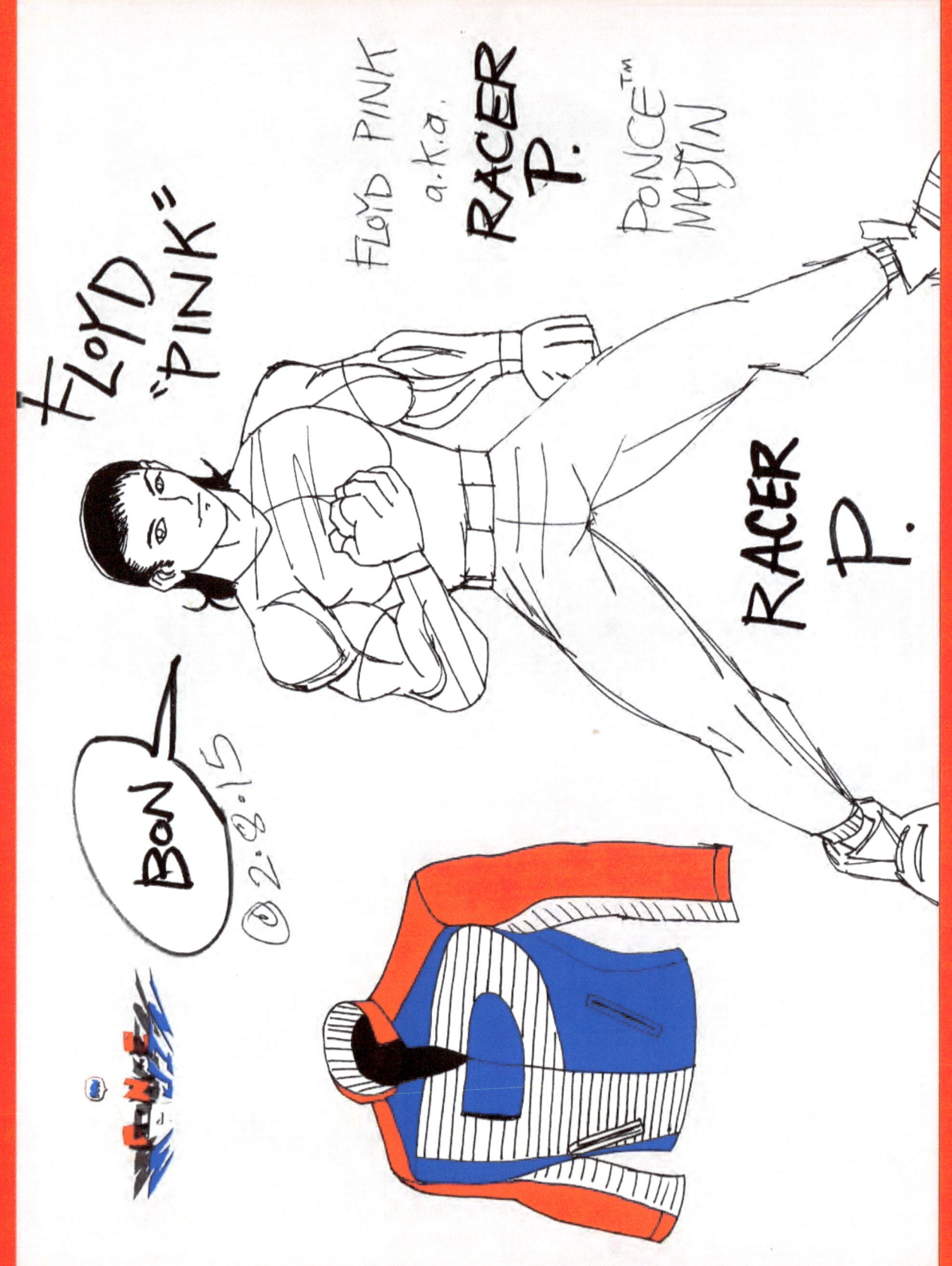

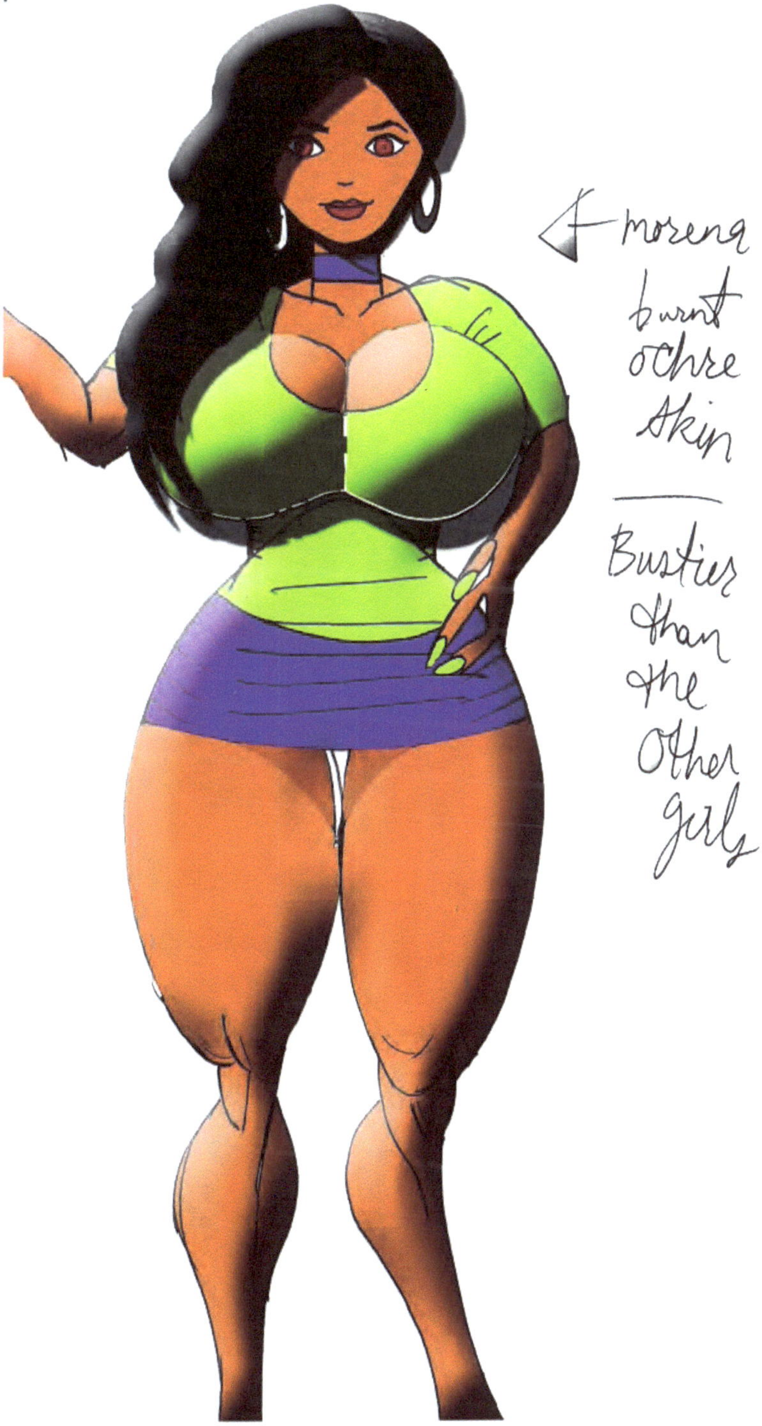

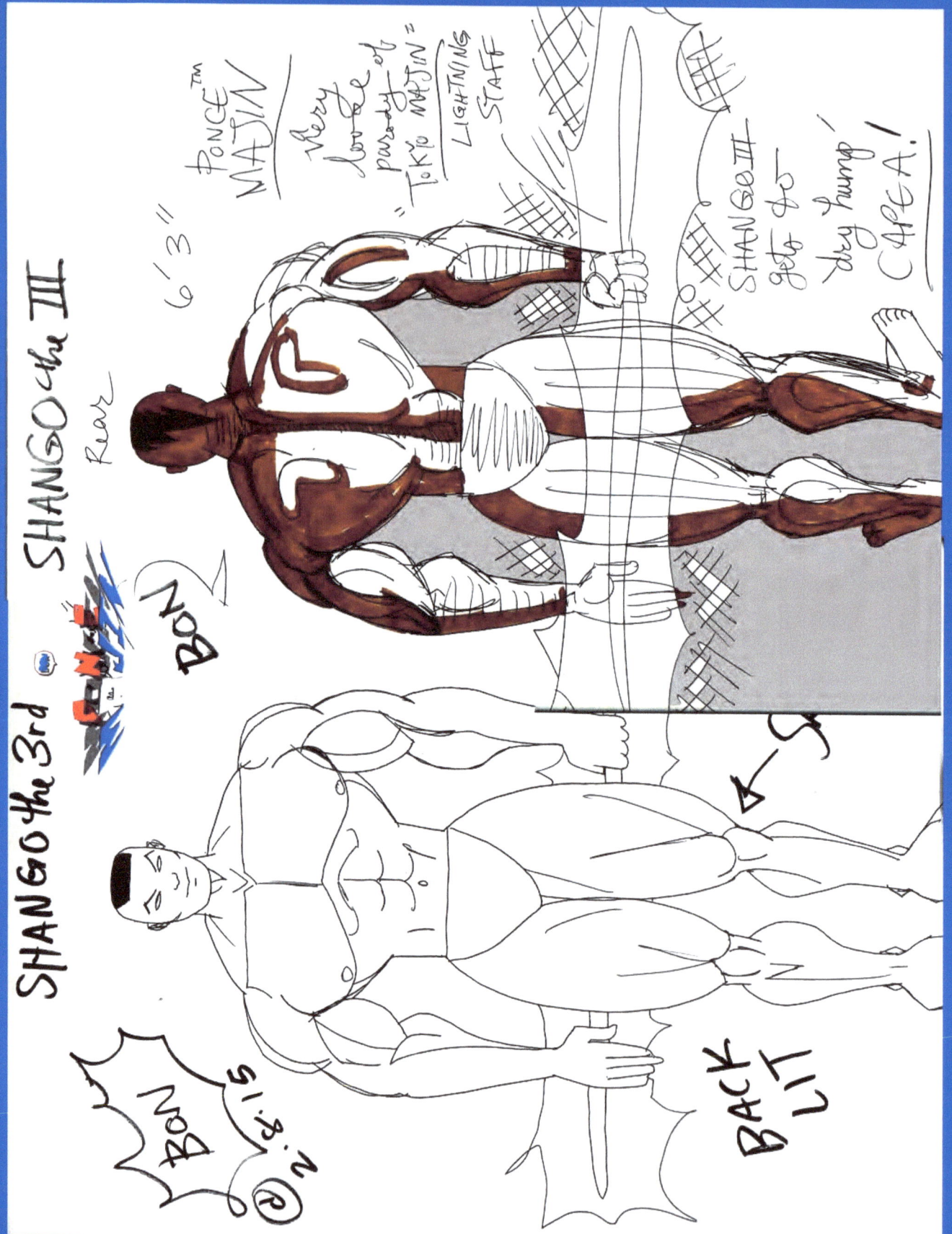

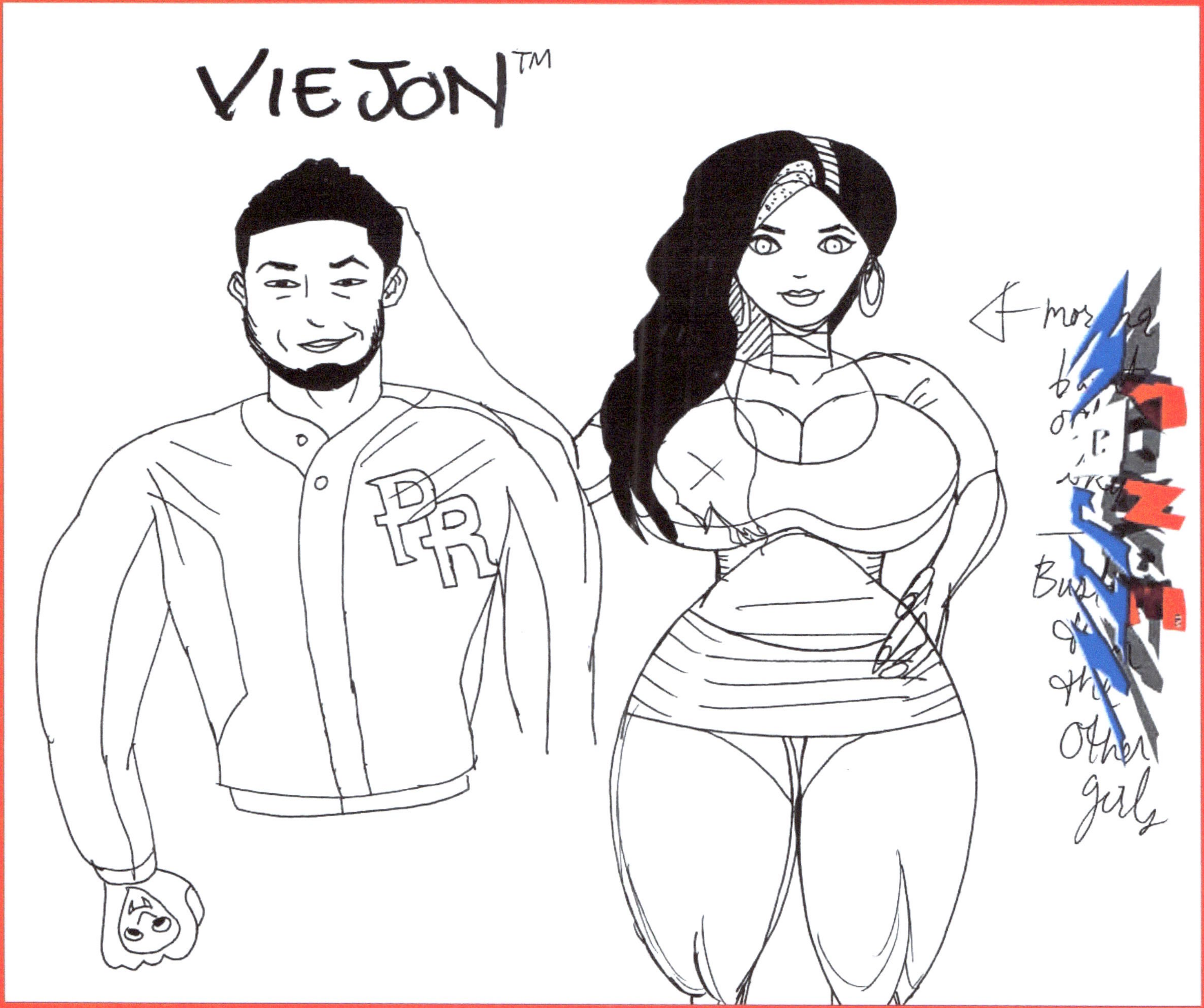

VANDALO OPRESO

NATIONALITY: (Latino) citizen of Belleza Reino with mysterious past, claims to be a vassal.

MAGIC: Vandalo is a master of illusion. However, he can project different realities to different people. Thus, he cannot project group hypnosis. He cannot give two or more people the same altered perception of reality. He takes Capea to his castle, but tells her not to invite her friends. That is because he cannot project the same illusions into the minds of multiple people. His magic only works one-on-one. He uses his magic to lie to young, beautiful women.

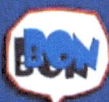

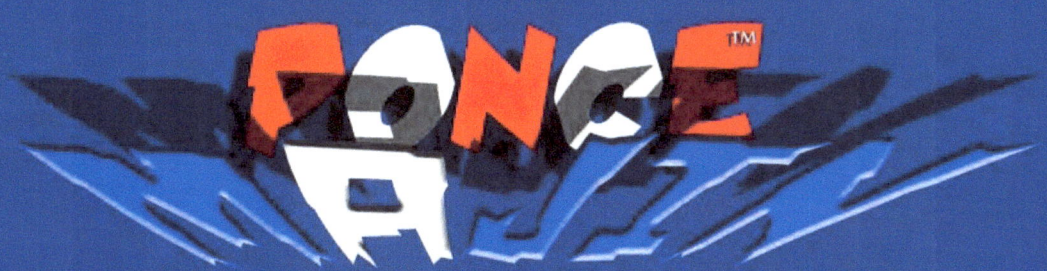

Episodes: 6

"69 PROBLEMS"

NO SEXY TIMES FOR SOMEONE

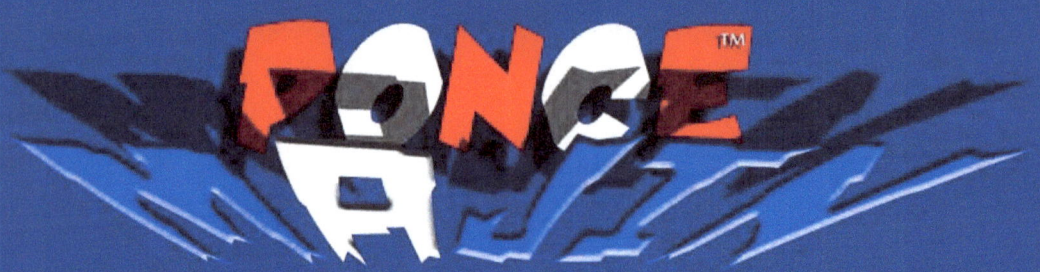

Episodes: 7
"BUNNY & TIGER!"

IN **THIS** CORNER:
MARCH HARE!

IN **THAT** CORNER:
TIGER-FOOL!

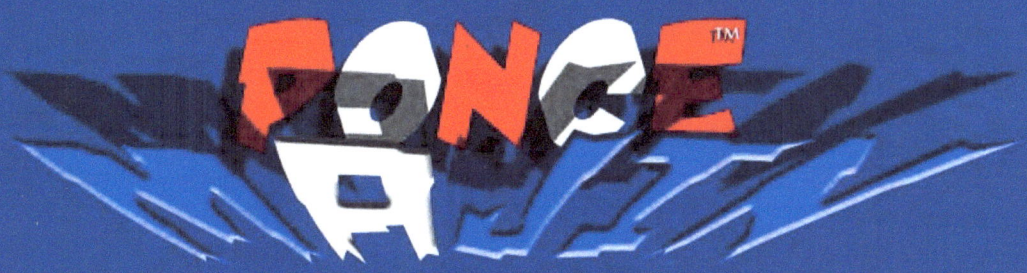

Episodes: 9

"SOMETHING LAGANN"

WHAT THE HELL DO YOU THINK?

UH, **GIANT ROBOTS** MUCH?
MECHS
MOBILE TANK POLICE?
BUBBLE GUM
&
CRISIS

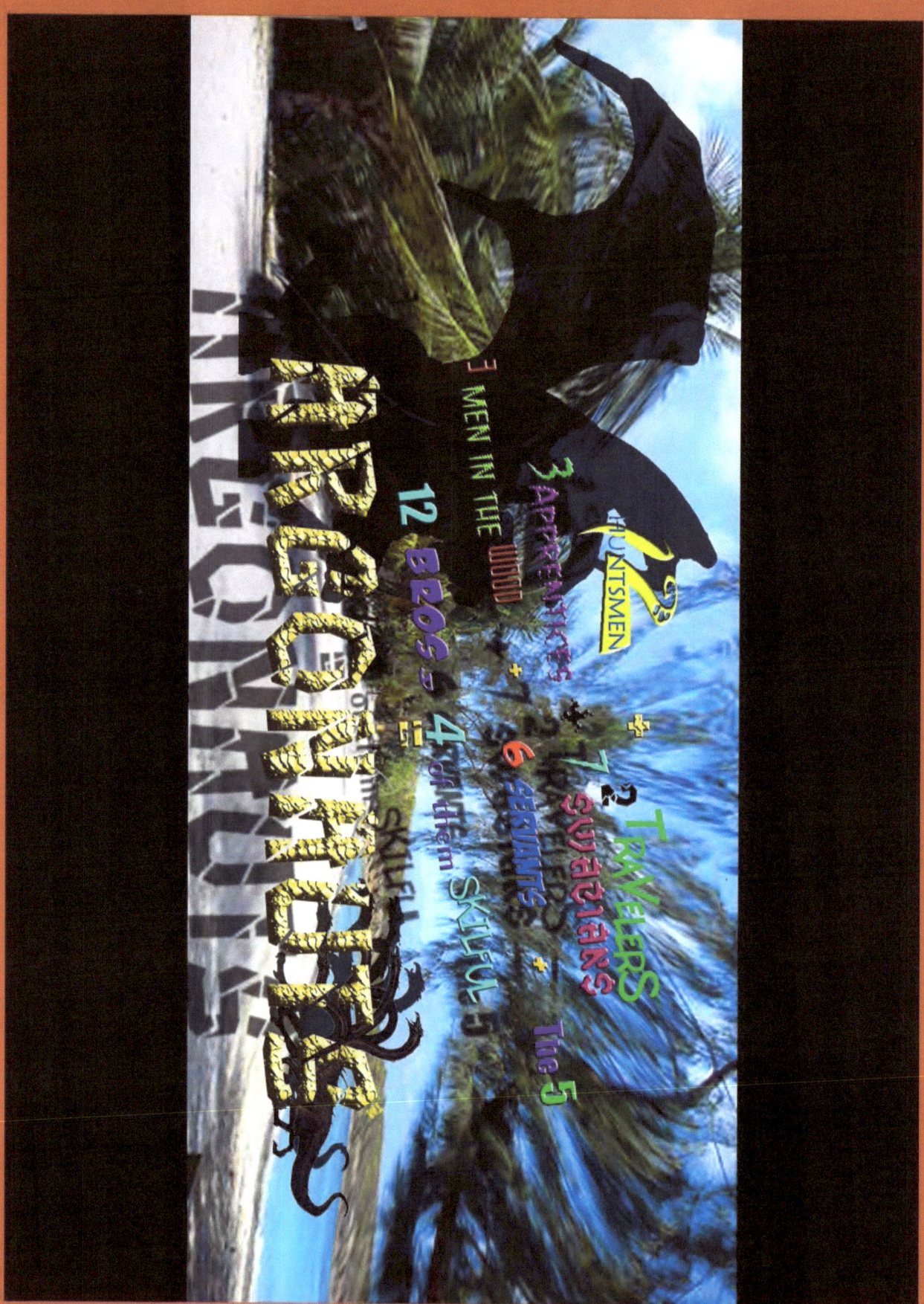

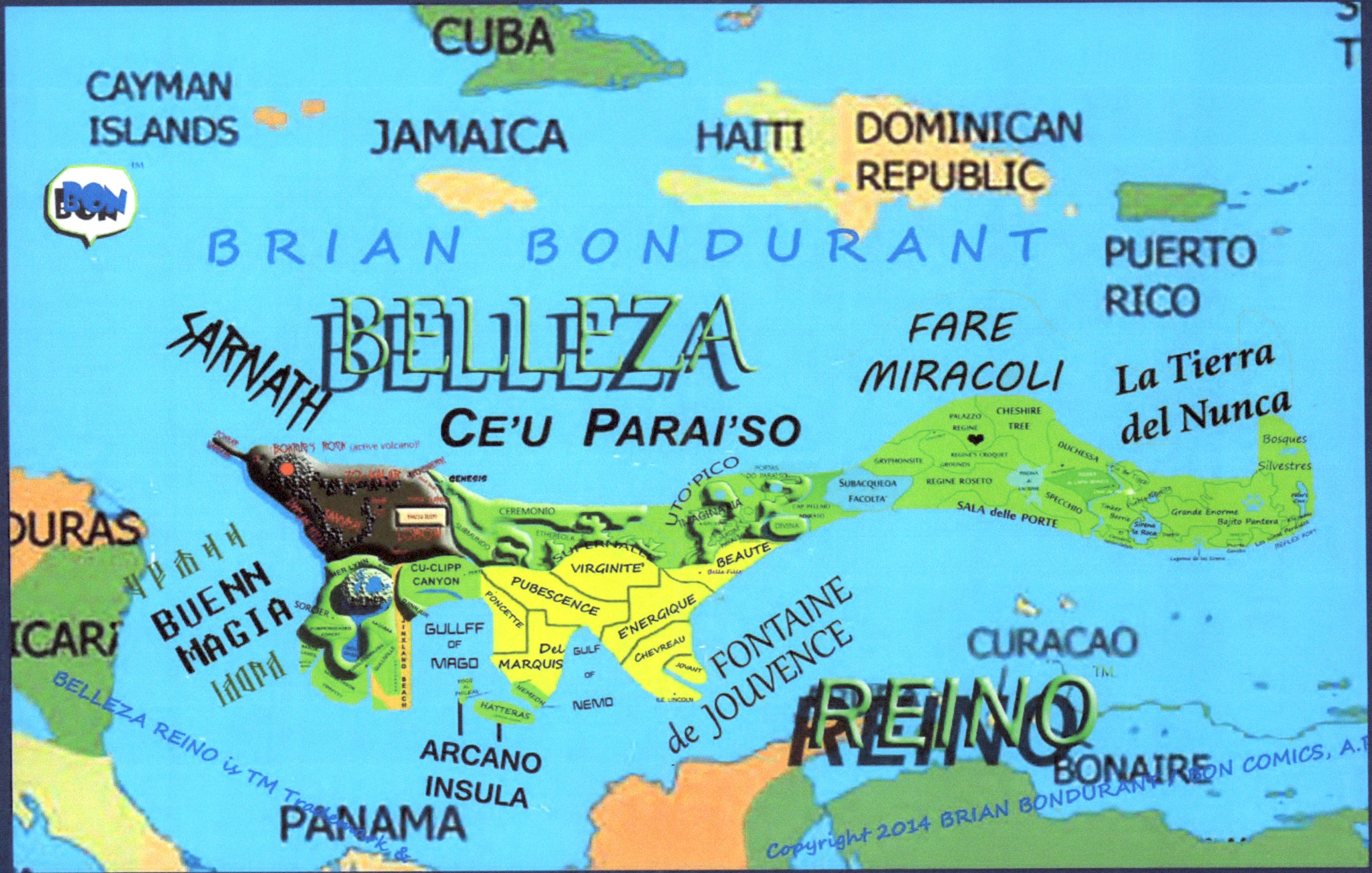
CUBA
CAYMAN ISLANDS
JAMAICA
HAITI
DOMINICAN REPUBLIC
PUERTO RICO
BRIAN BONDURANT
BELLEZA
SARNATH
CE'U PARAI'SO
FARE MIRACOLI
La Tierra del Nunca
UTO'PICO
CU-CLIPP CANYON
VIRGINITE'
PUBESCENCE
BEAUTE
E'NERGIQUE
CHEVREAU
PONCETTE
GULLFF OF MAGO
Del MARQUIS
GULF OF NEMO
NEMO
HATTERAS
ARCANO INSULA
BUENN MAGIA
FONTAINE de JOUVENCE
CURACAO
REINO
BONAIRE
PANAMA
SUBACQUEOA FACOLTA'
REGINE ROSETO
SALA delle PORTE
CHESHIRE TREE
DUCHESSA
SPECCHIO
Grande Enorme
Bajito Pantera
Bosques Silvestres
CEREMONIO
BELLEZA REINO is TM Trademark &
Copyright 2014 BRIAN BONDURANT BON COMICS, A.

Island Nation Flags

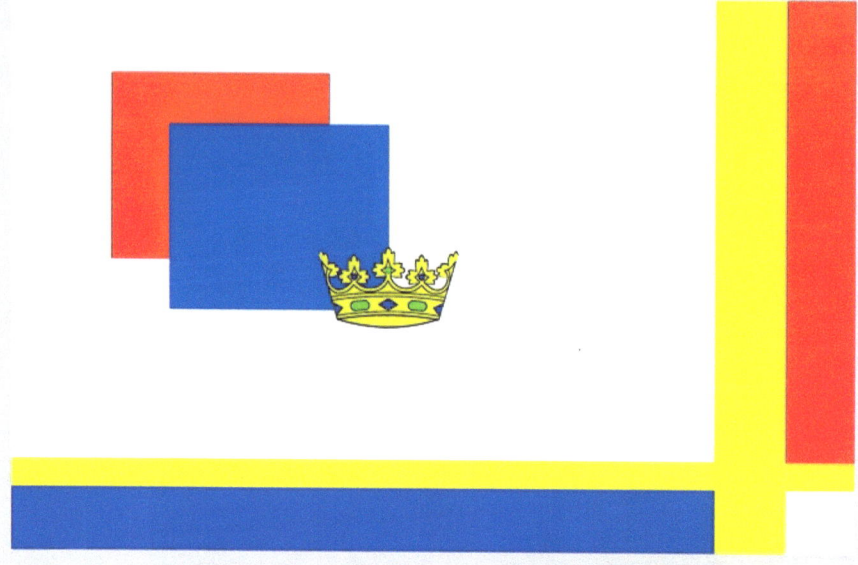

BELLEZA REINO

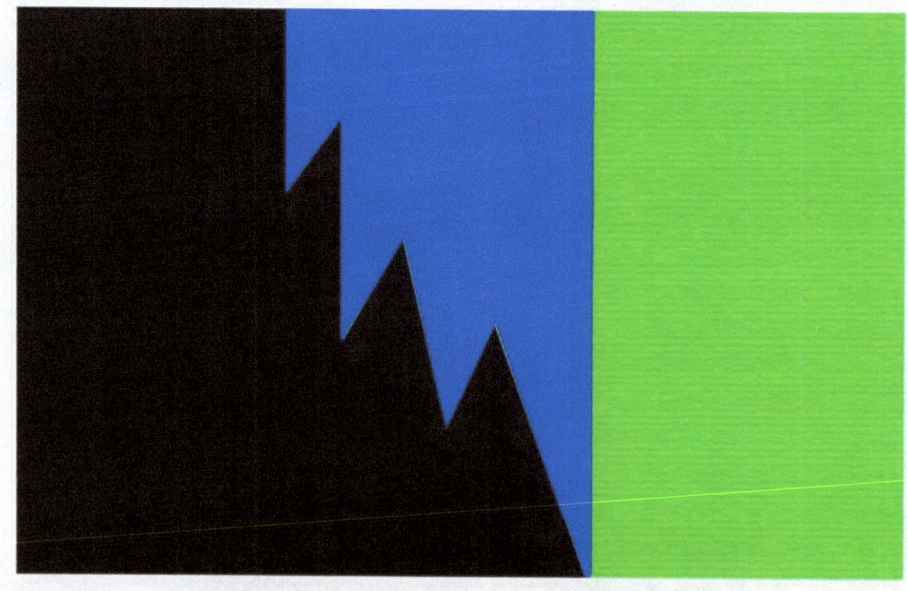

MERBSYLVEBUE

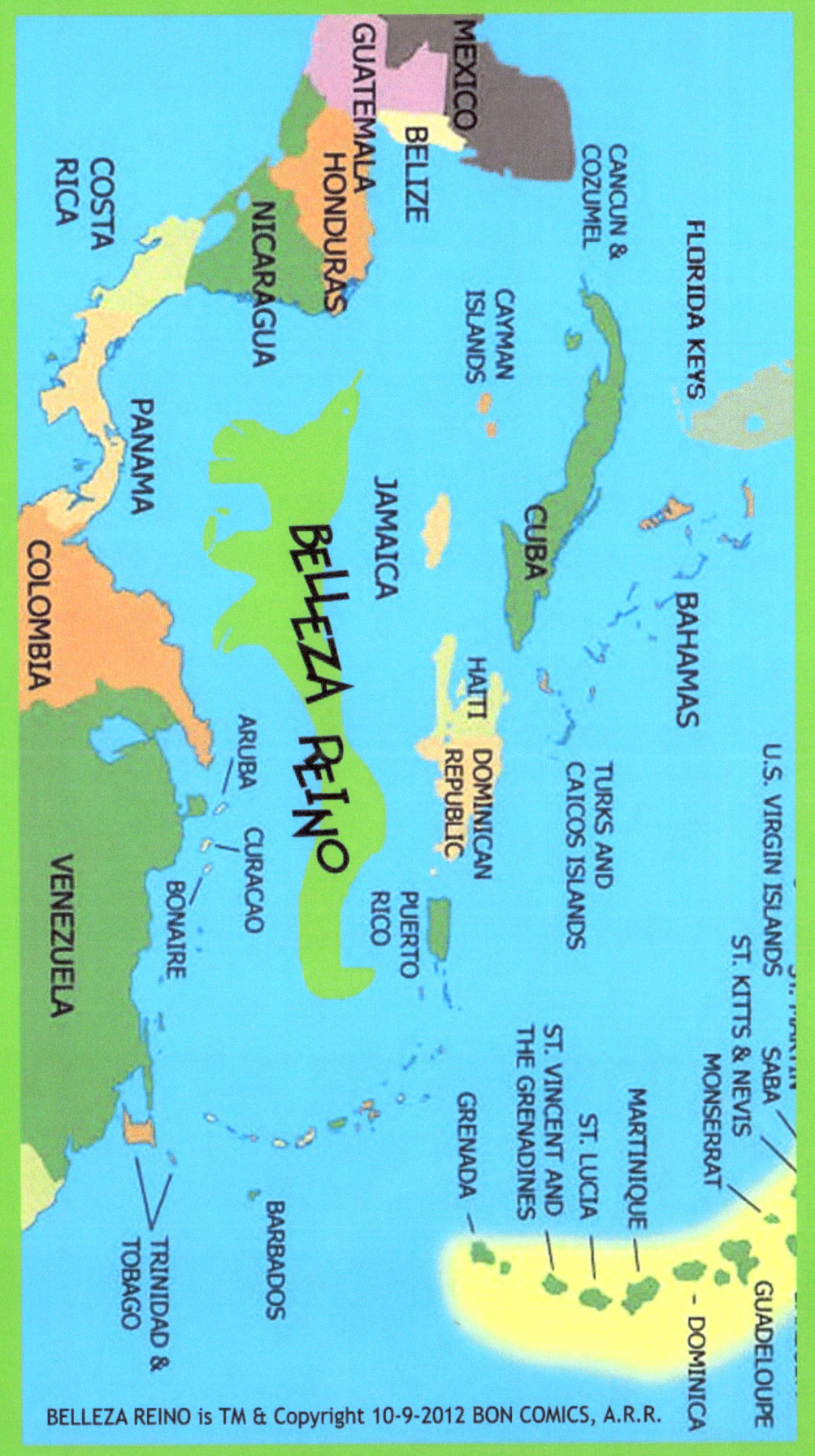

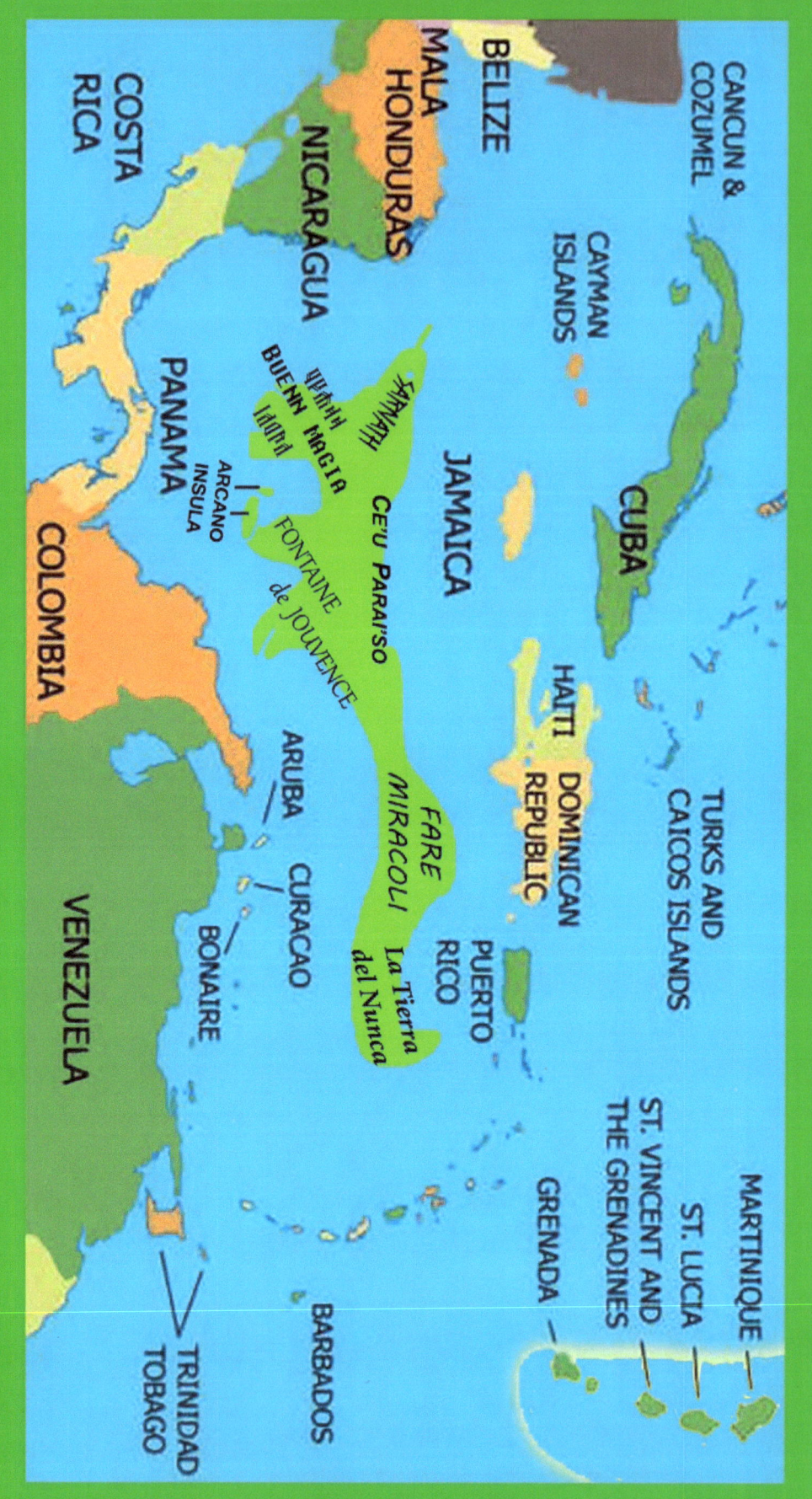

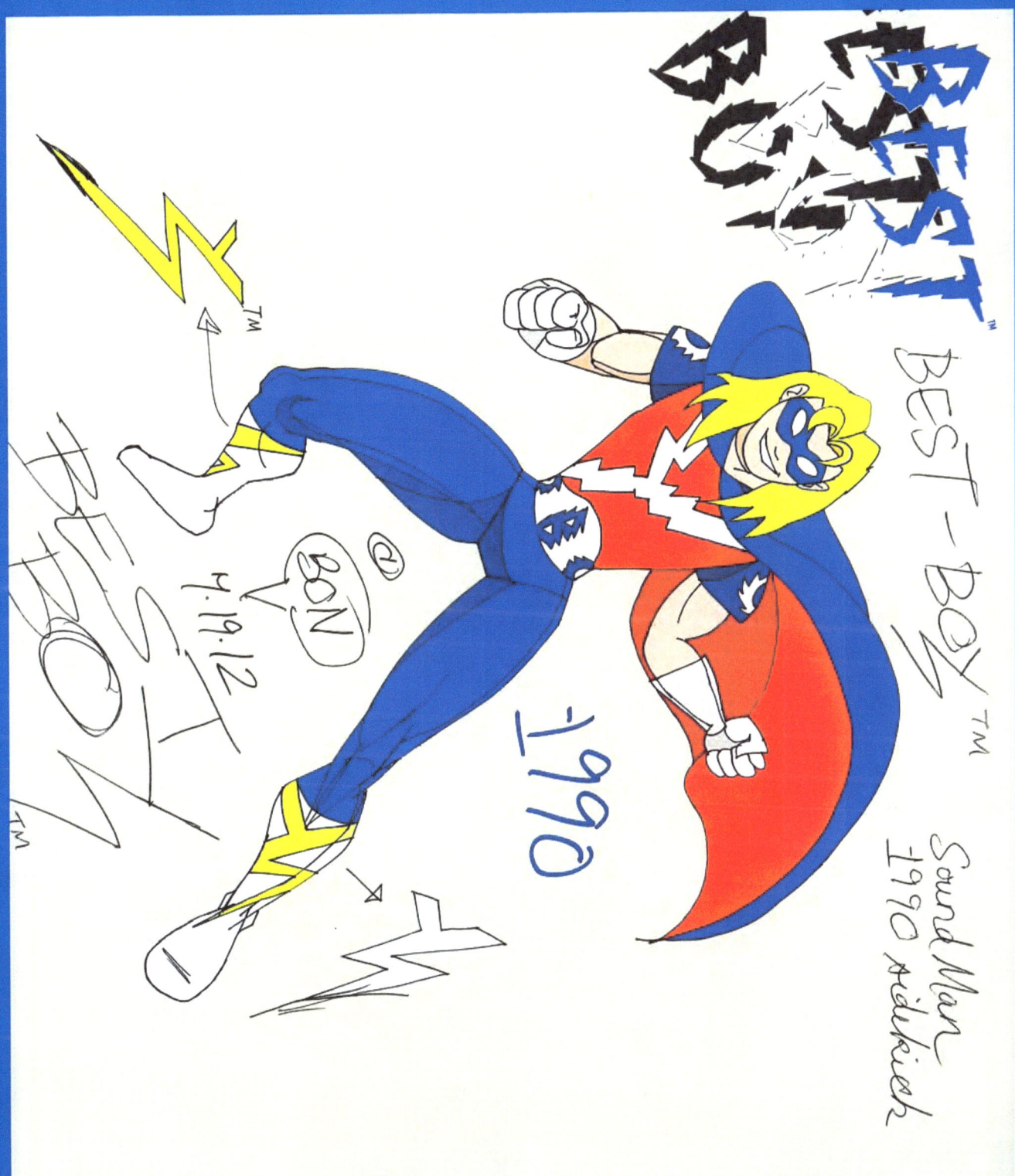

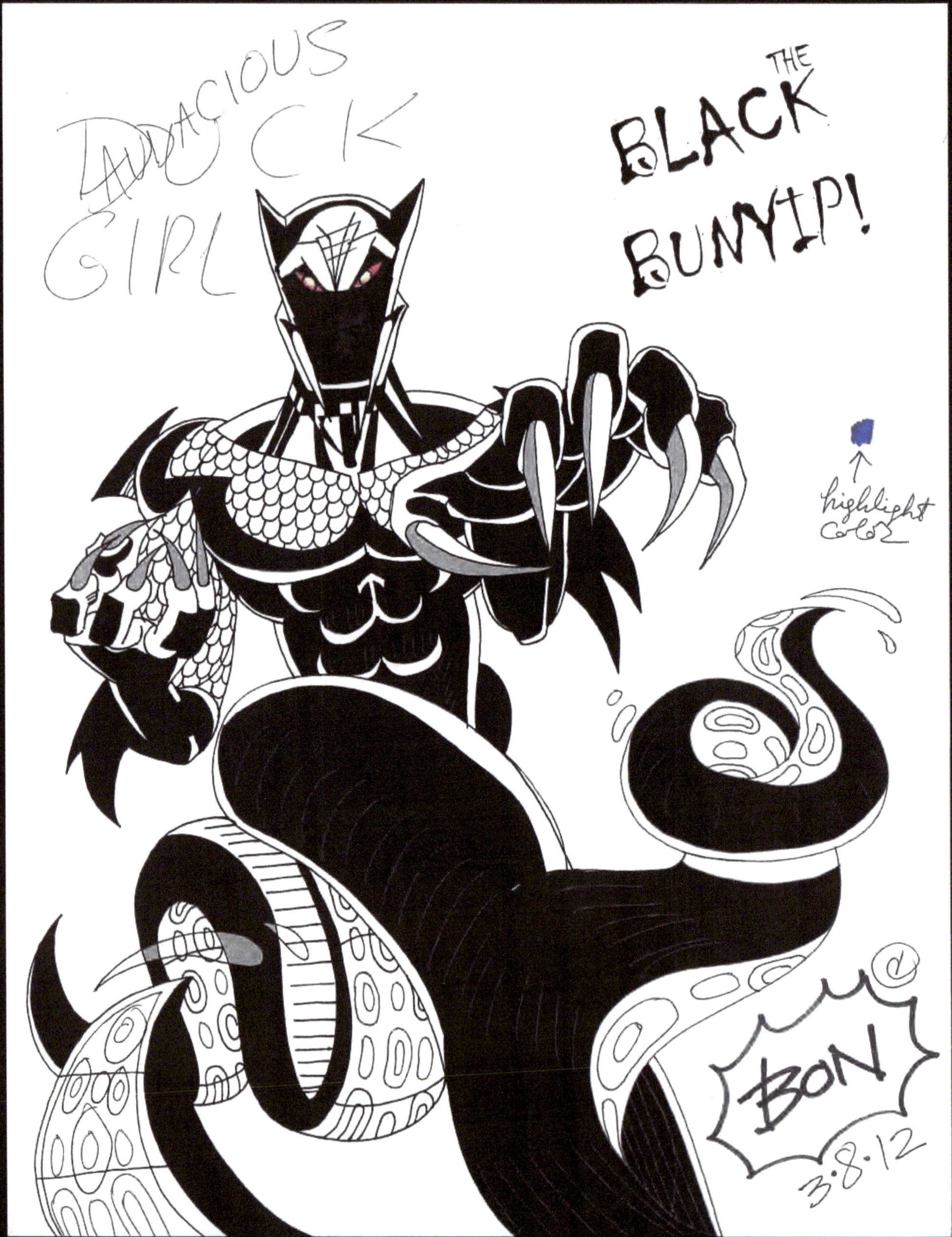

AUDACIOUS
DUCK
GIRL
THE BLACK BUNYIP!
highlight color
BON
3.8.12

BON COMICS GROUP™

$2.95
$4.70
CANADA
JUNE 2005

The
12
HUNTSMEN™

The
9 HUNTSMEN™

The
8 Huntsmen™

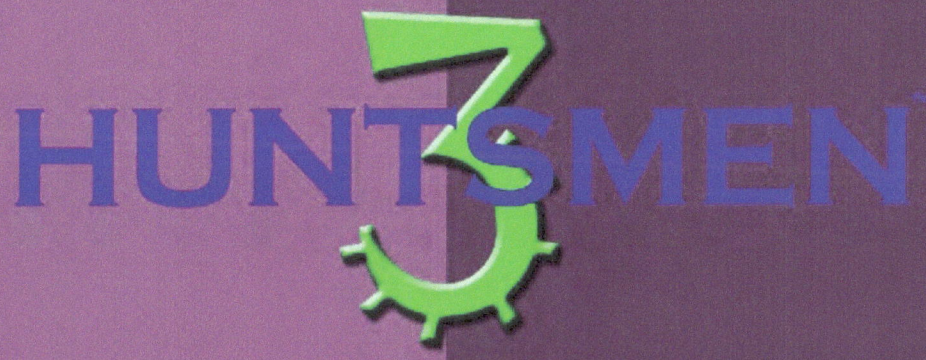

HUNTSMEN 3

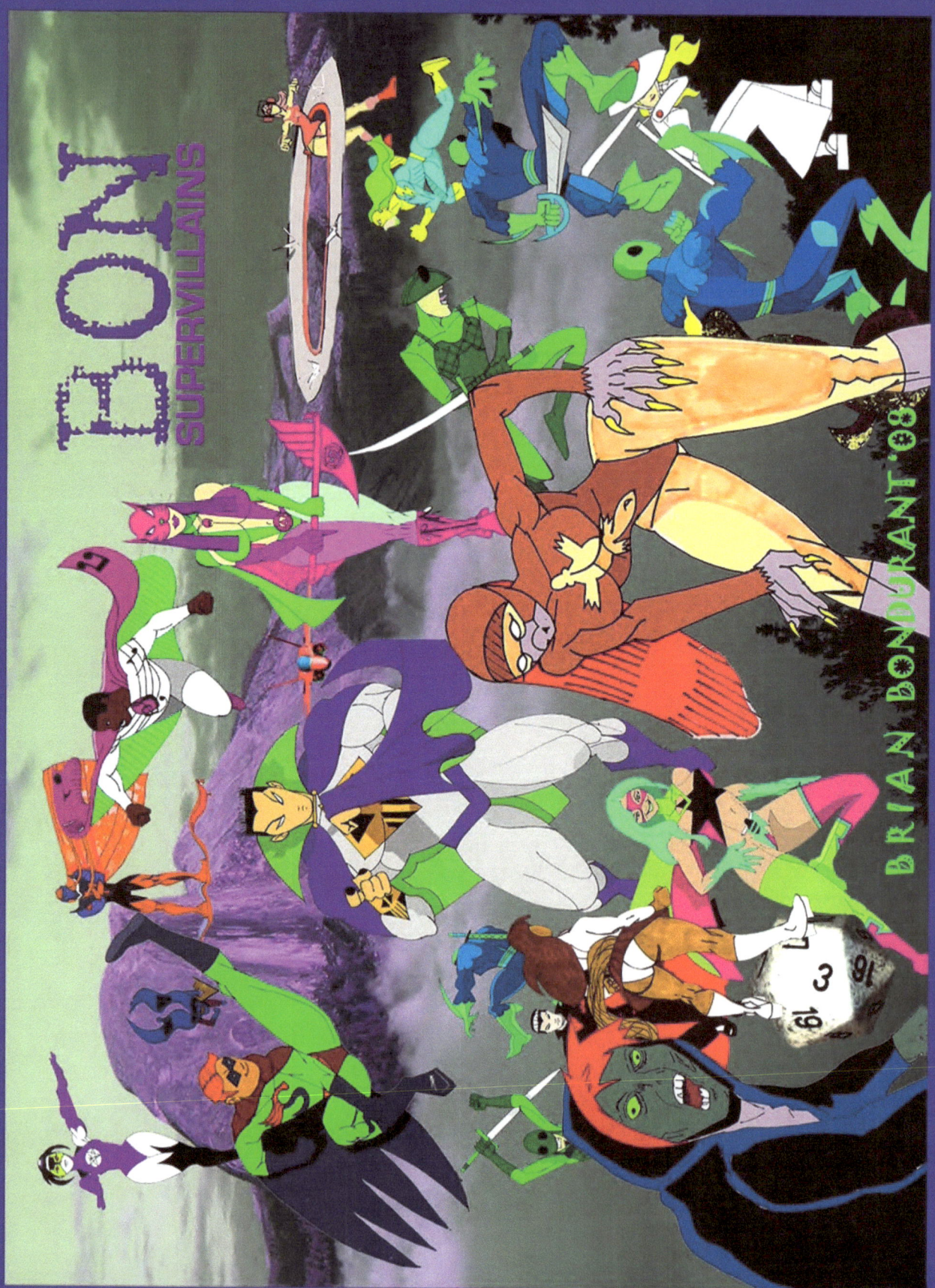

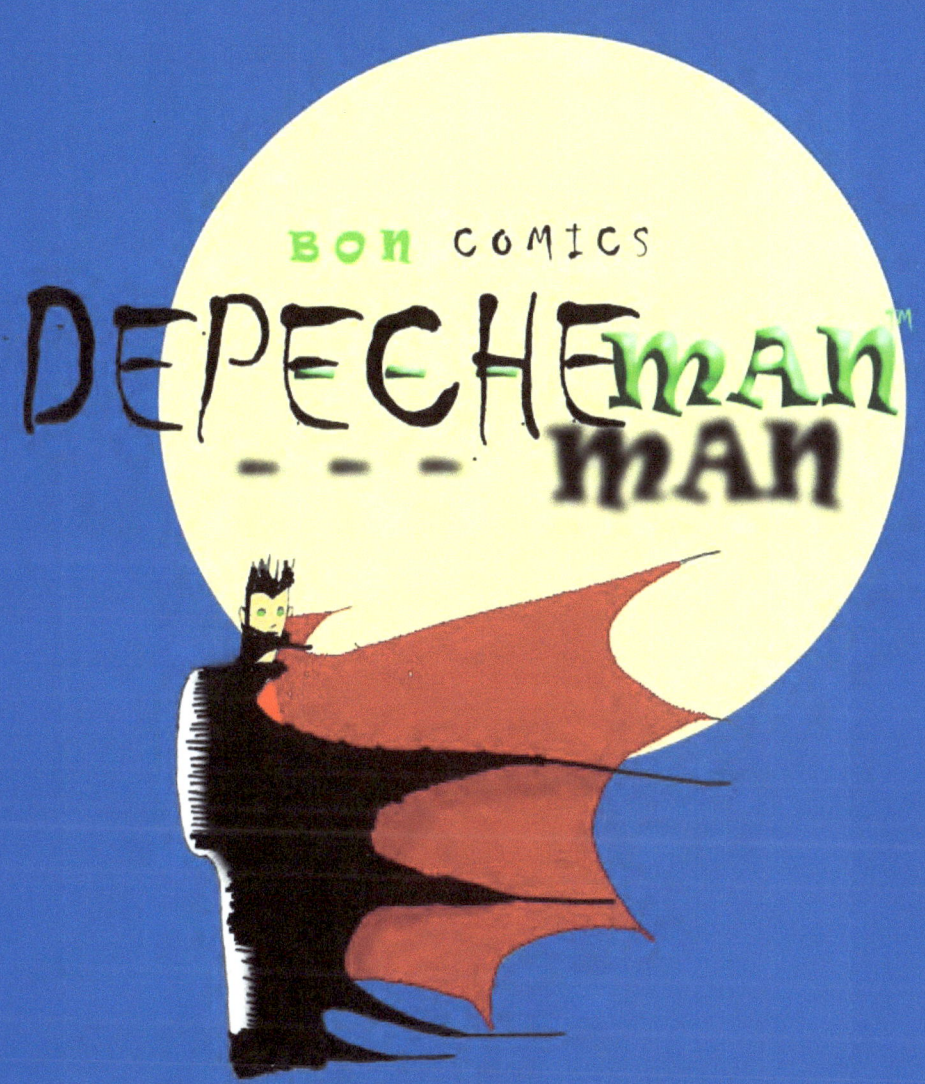

BON COMICS

DEPECHEMAN™
MAN™

Brian

Bondurant

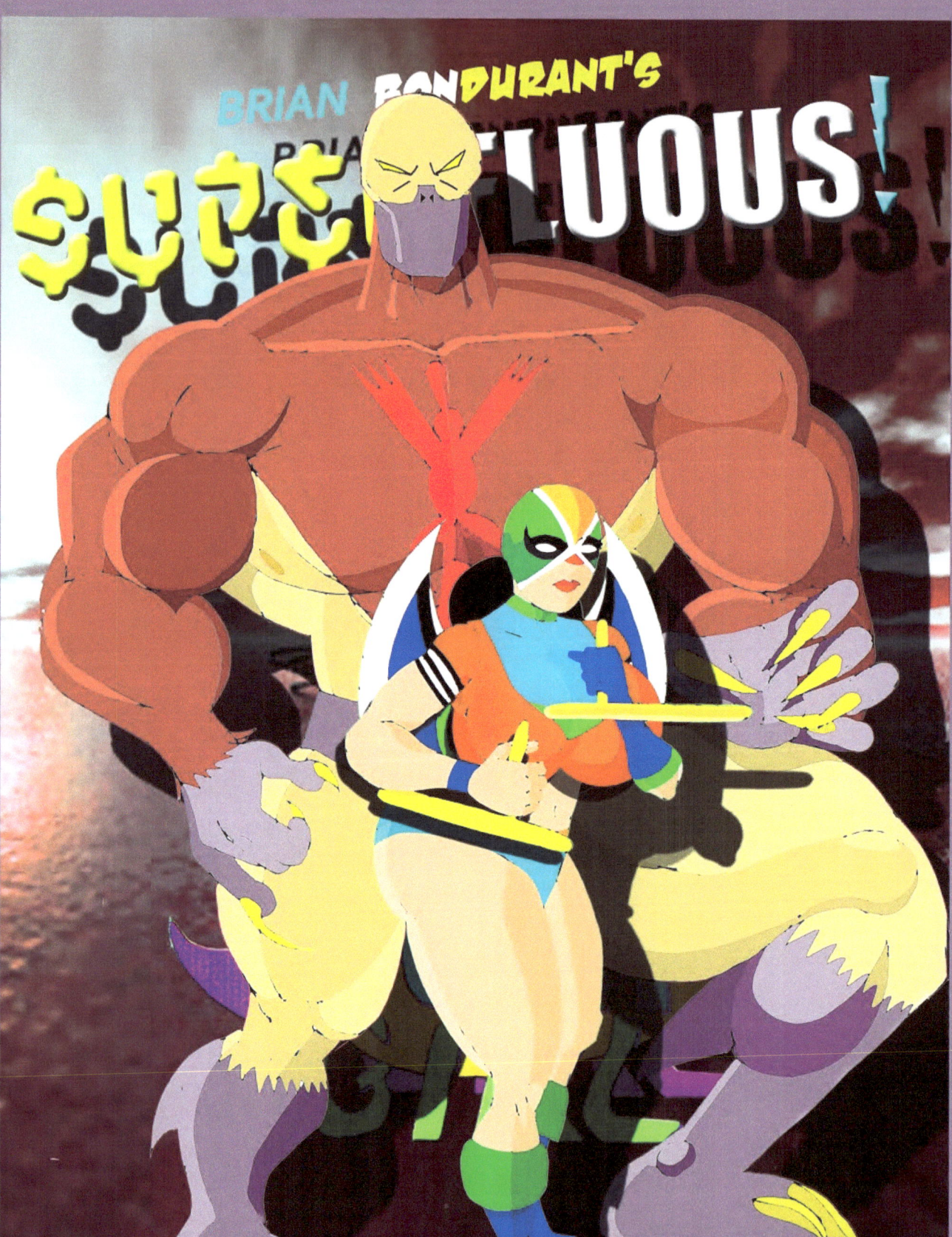

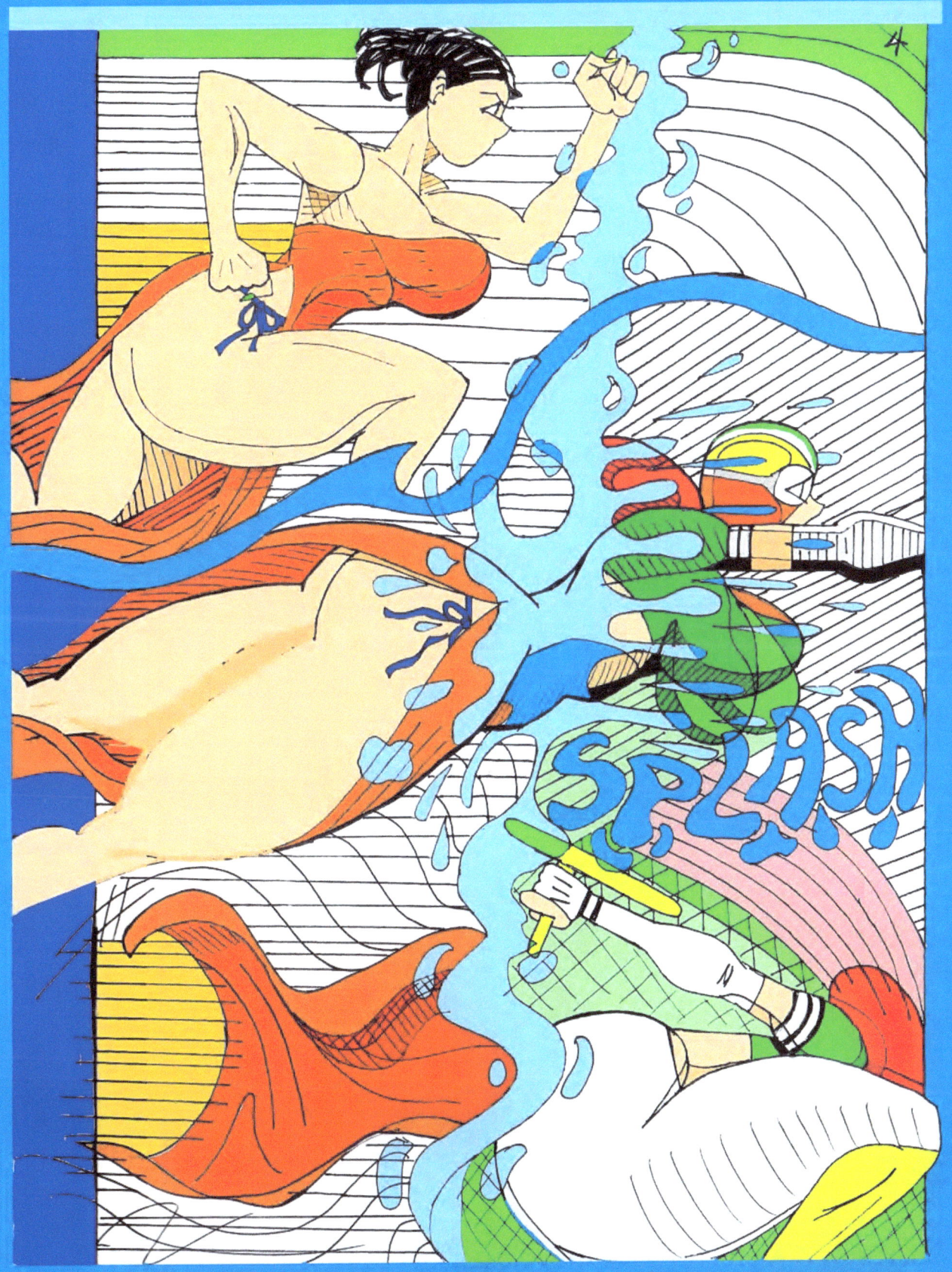

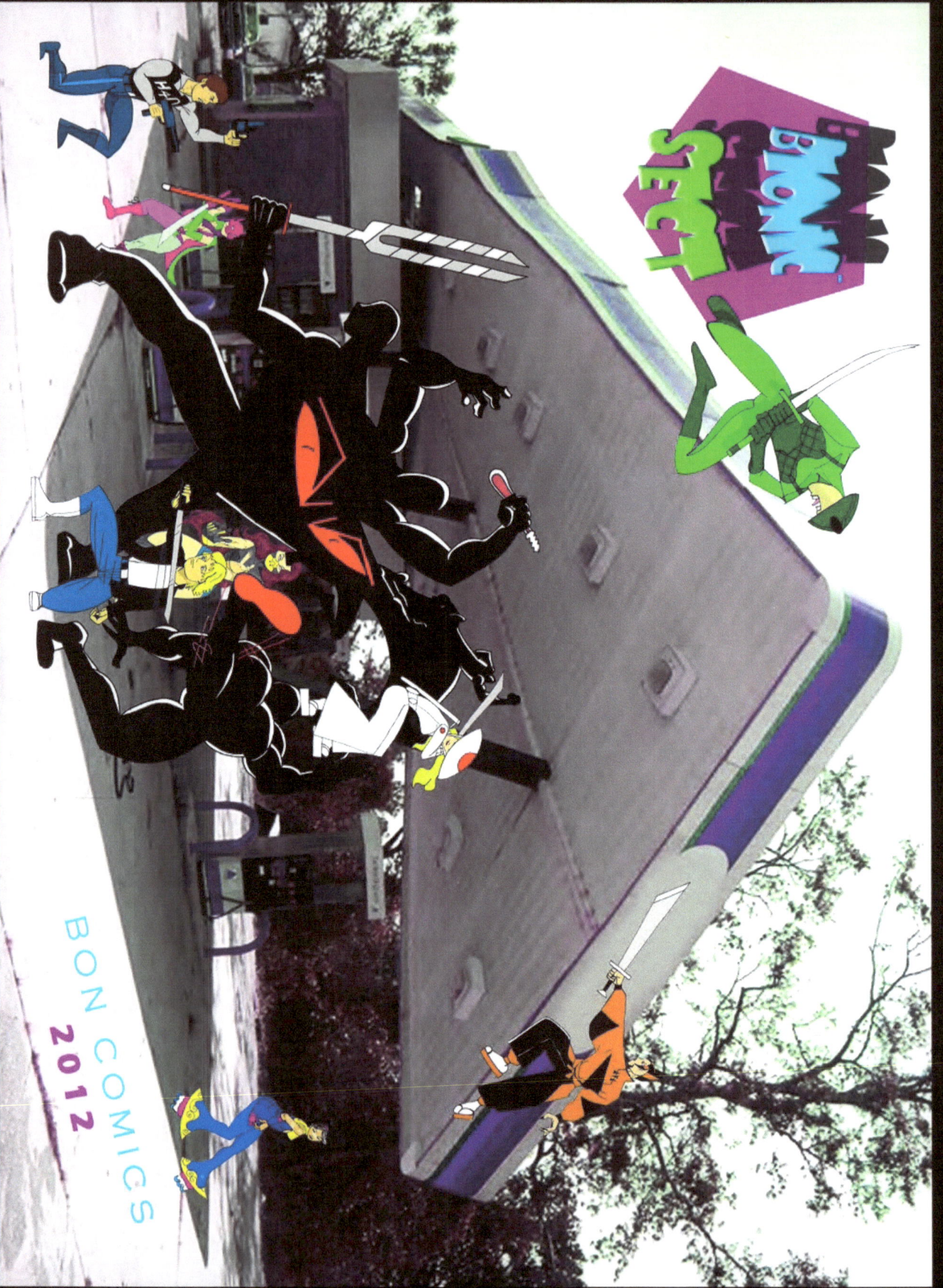

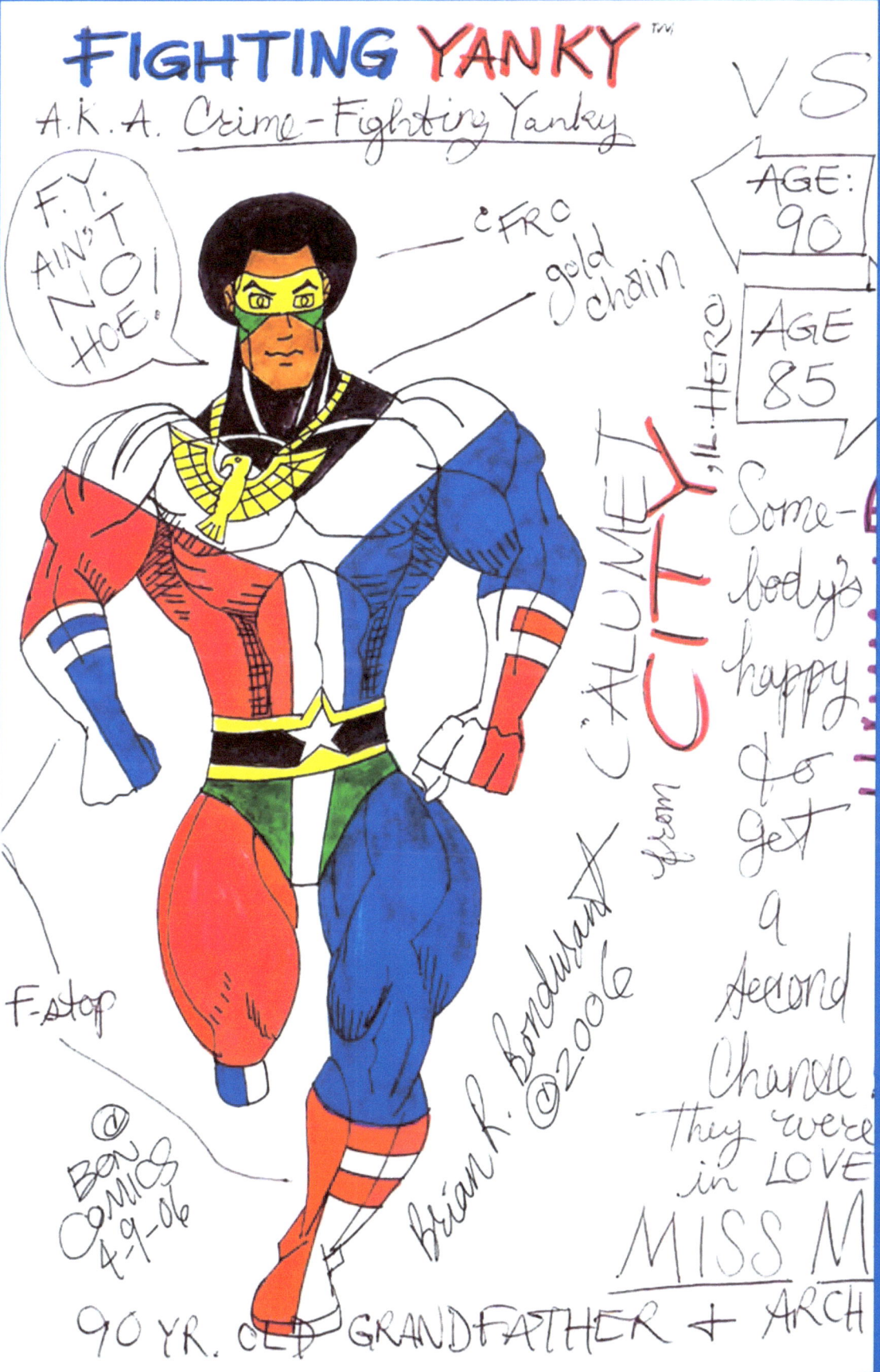

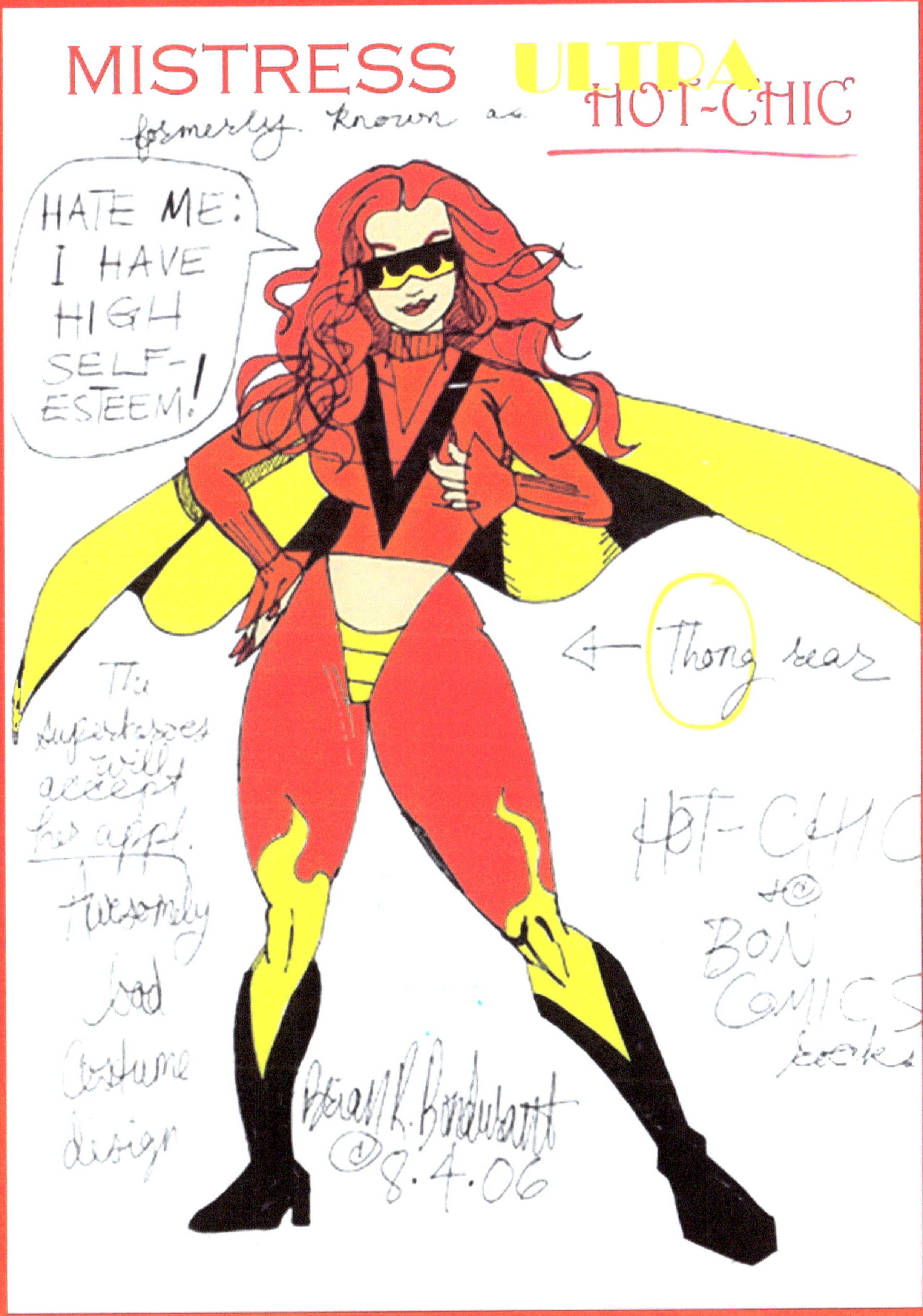
MISTRESS ULTRA
formerly known as
HOT-CHIC
HATE ME: I HAVE HIGH SELF-ESTEEM!
Thong rear
The superheroes will accept her appl.
Awesomely bad costume design
HOT-CHIC ©
BON COMICS books
Brian K. Bondurant © 8.4.06

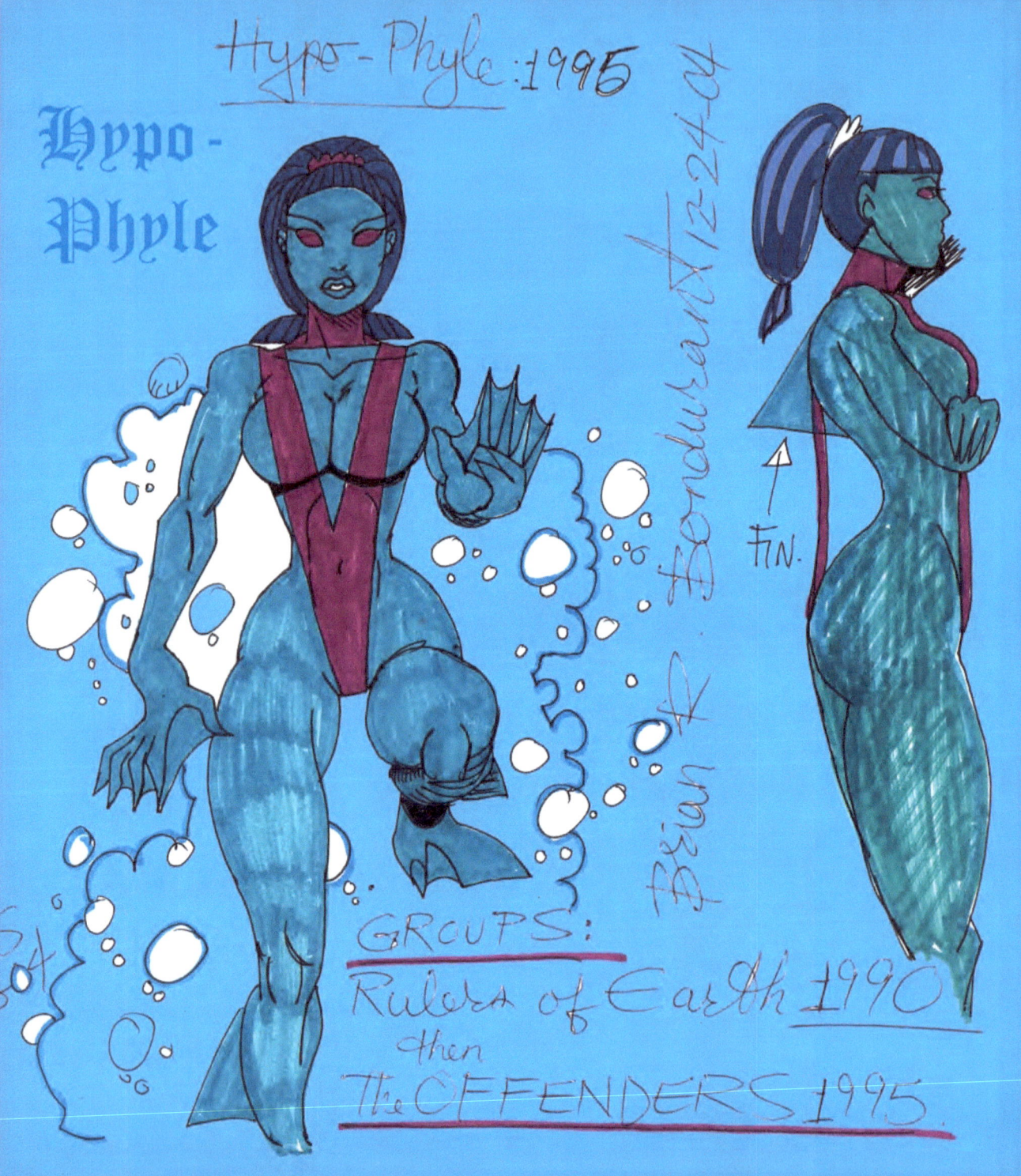

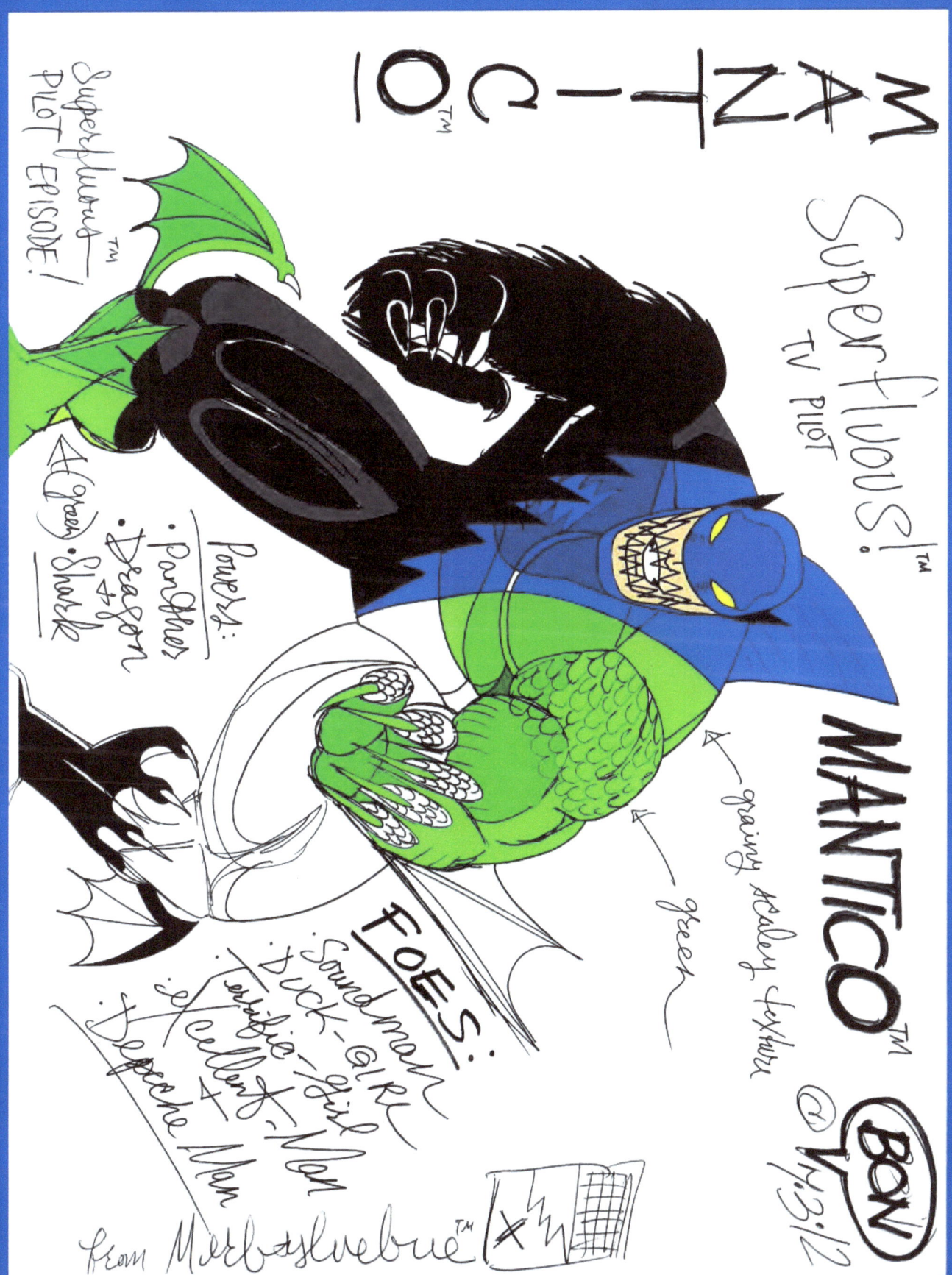

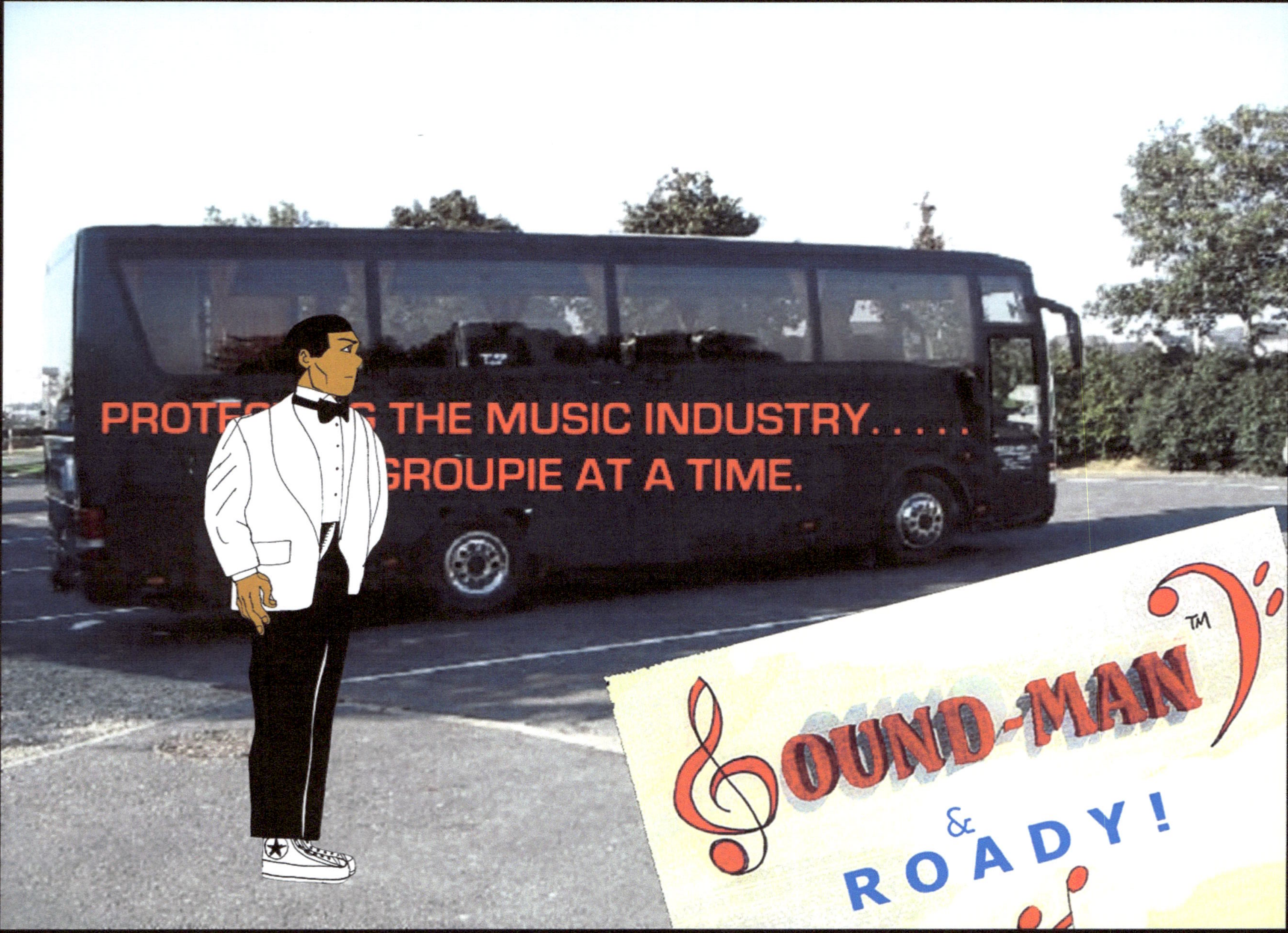
PROTE THE MUSIC INDUSTRY.....
GROUPIE AT A TIME.
OUND-MAN™
&
ROADY!

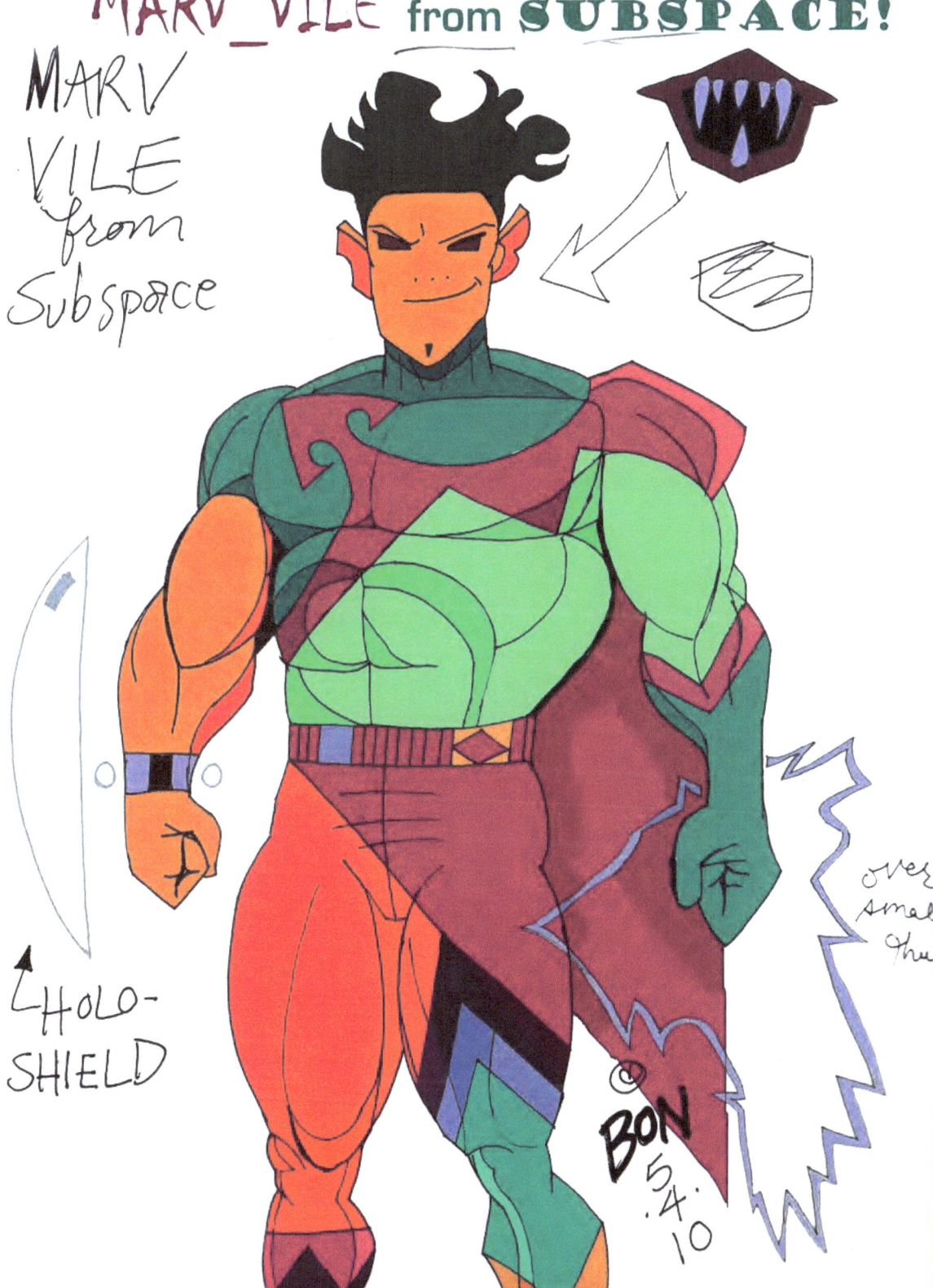

MASTERS of GOOD
UNIFY!!!

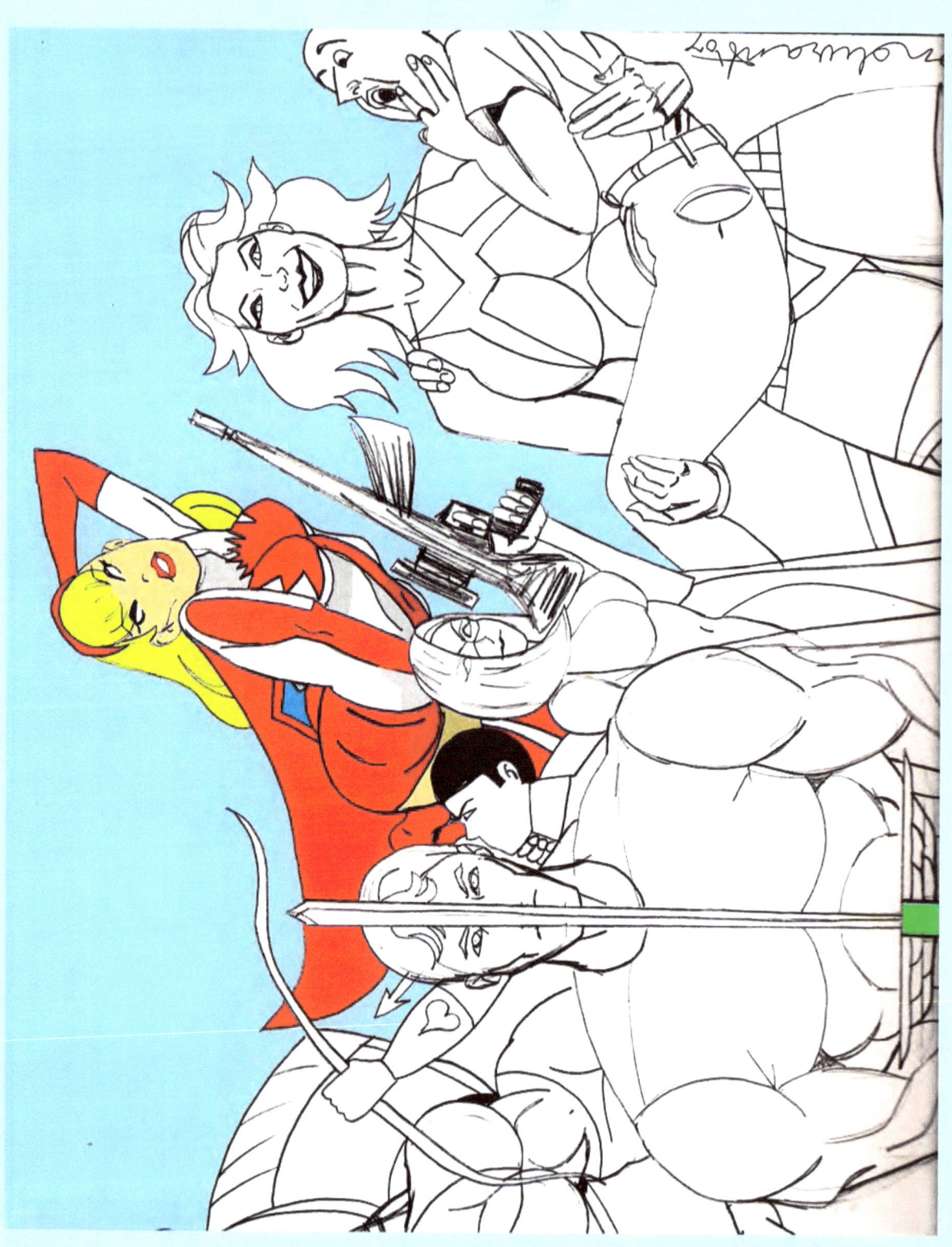

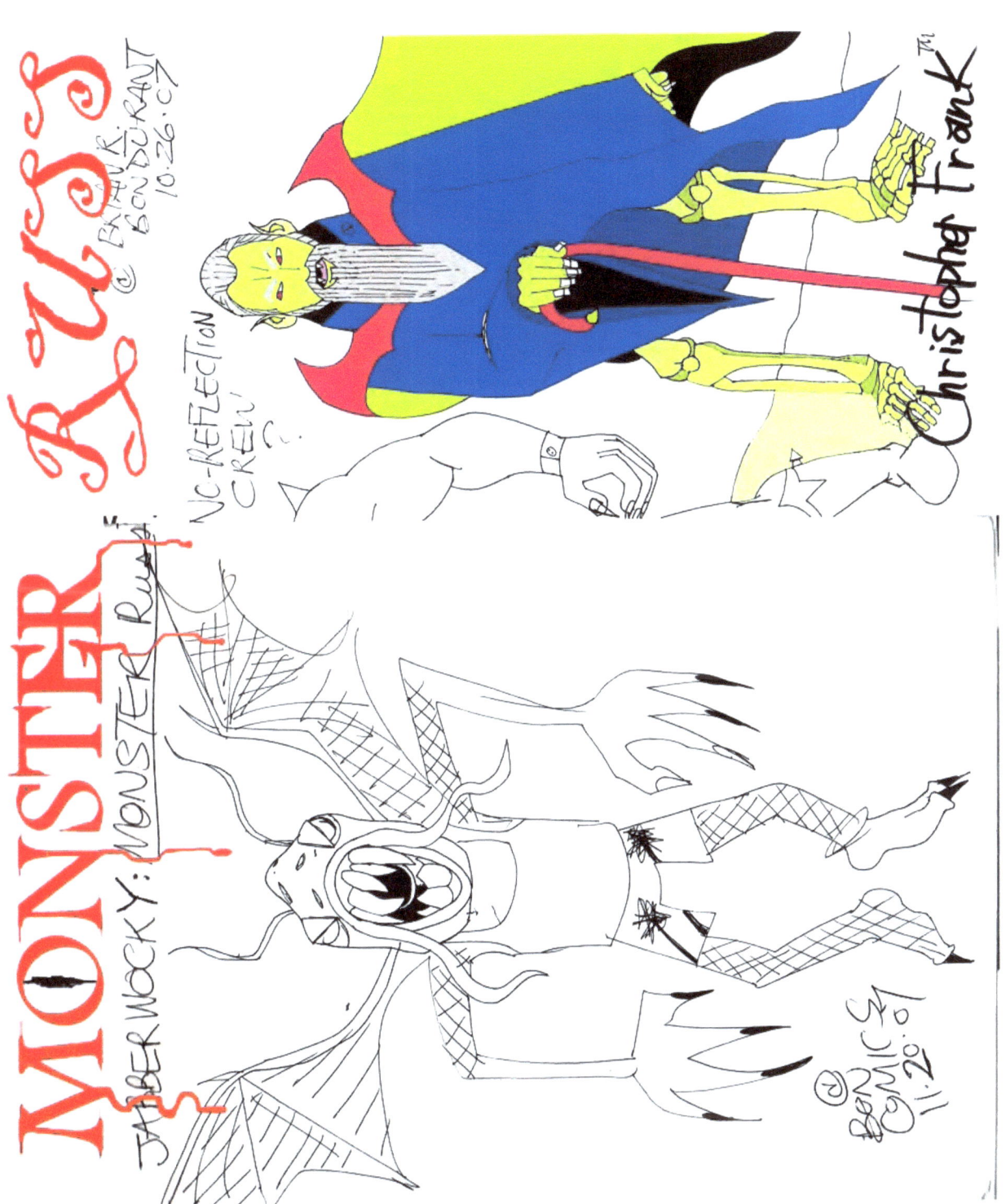

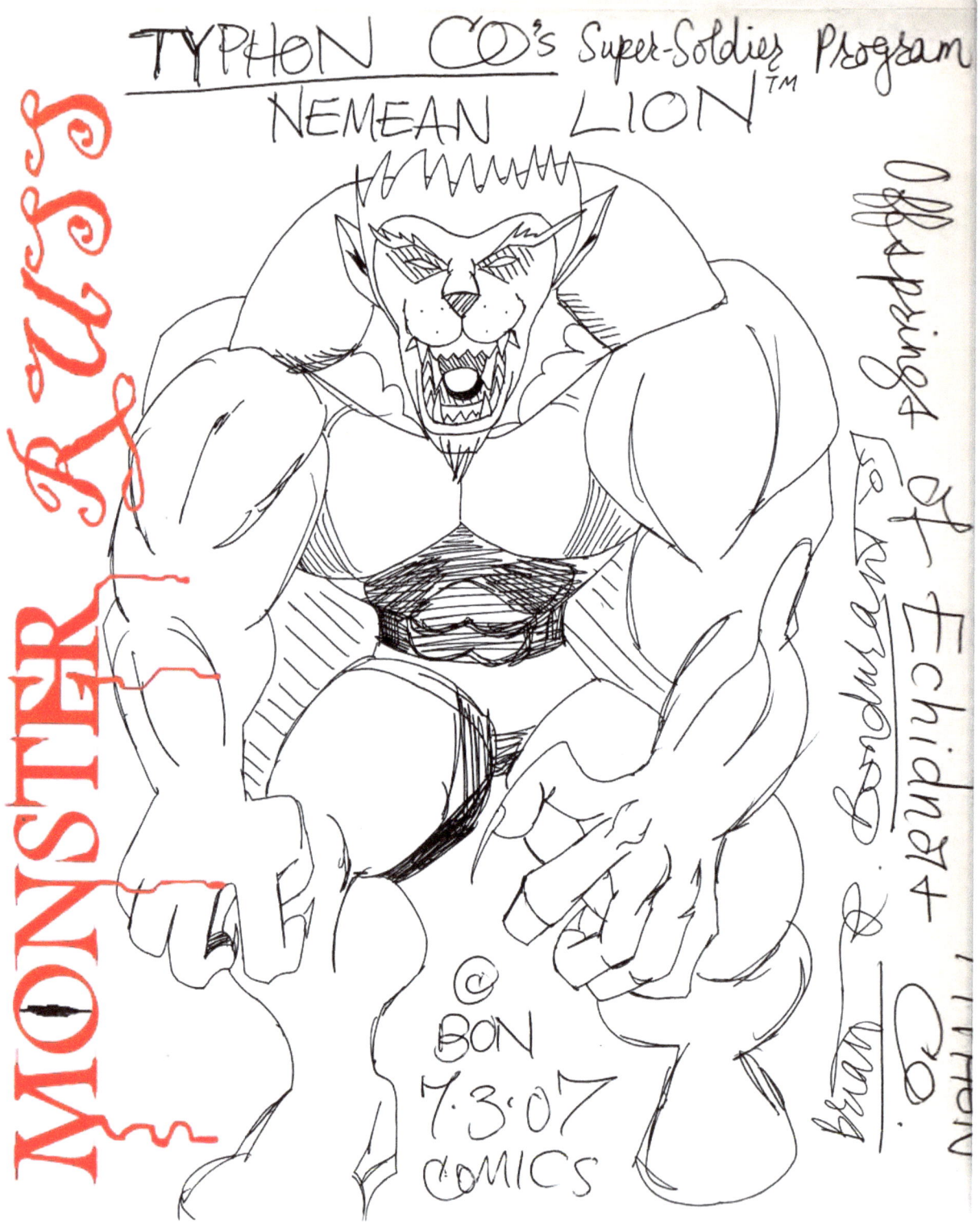

MONSTER RUSS

PETE the MADMAN : Monster Russ

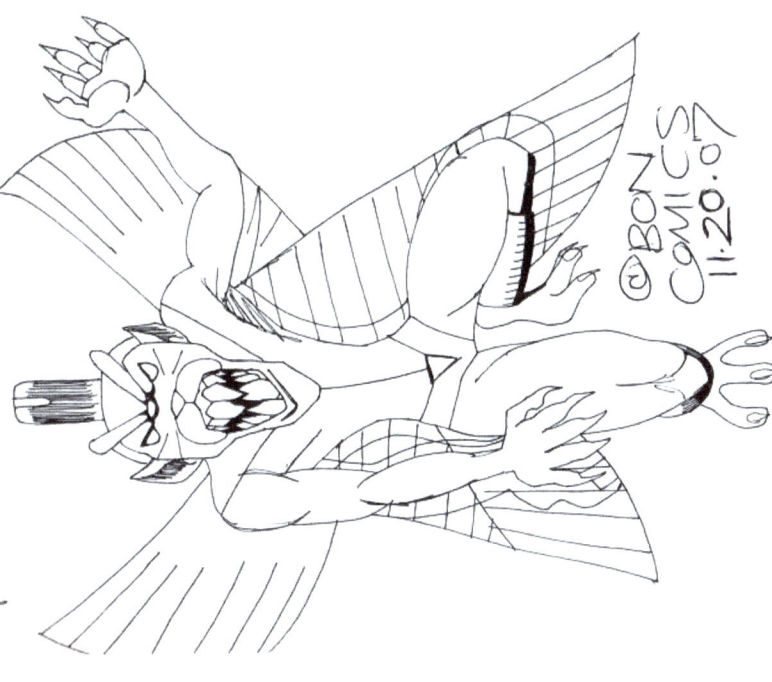

wave action hair

11-20-07 @ BoN COMICS

PAZUZU : "MONSTER RUSS"™

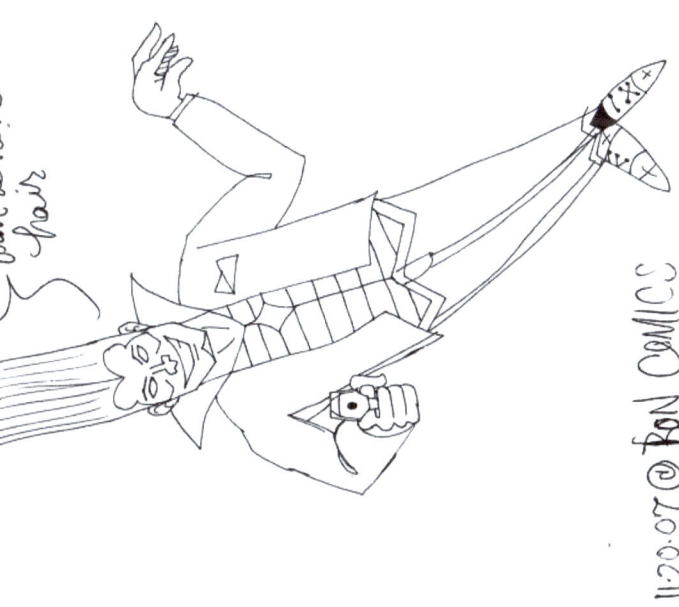

@ BON COMICS
11-20-07

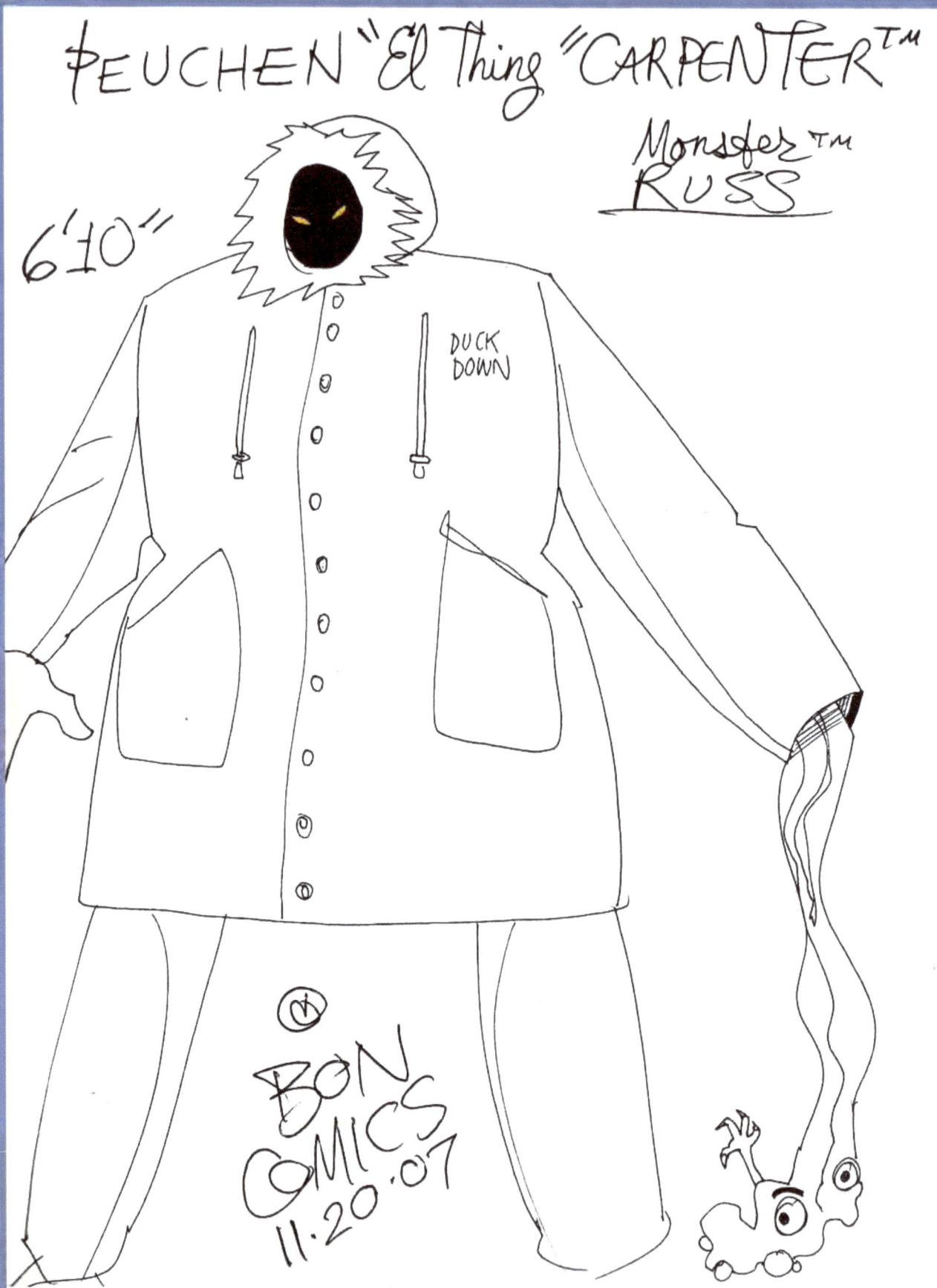

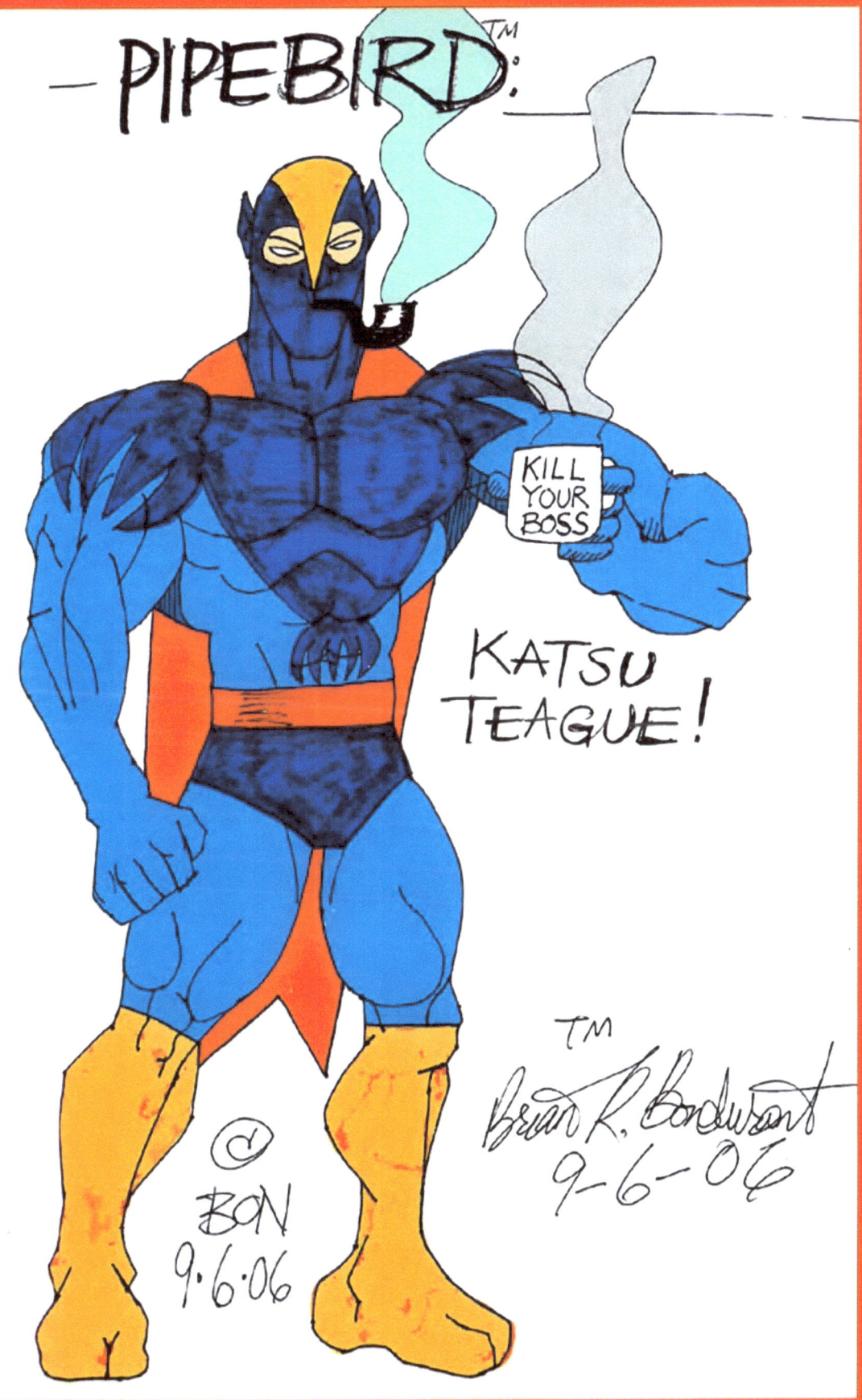

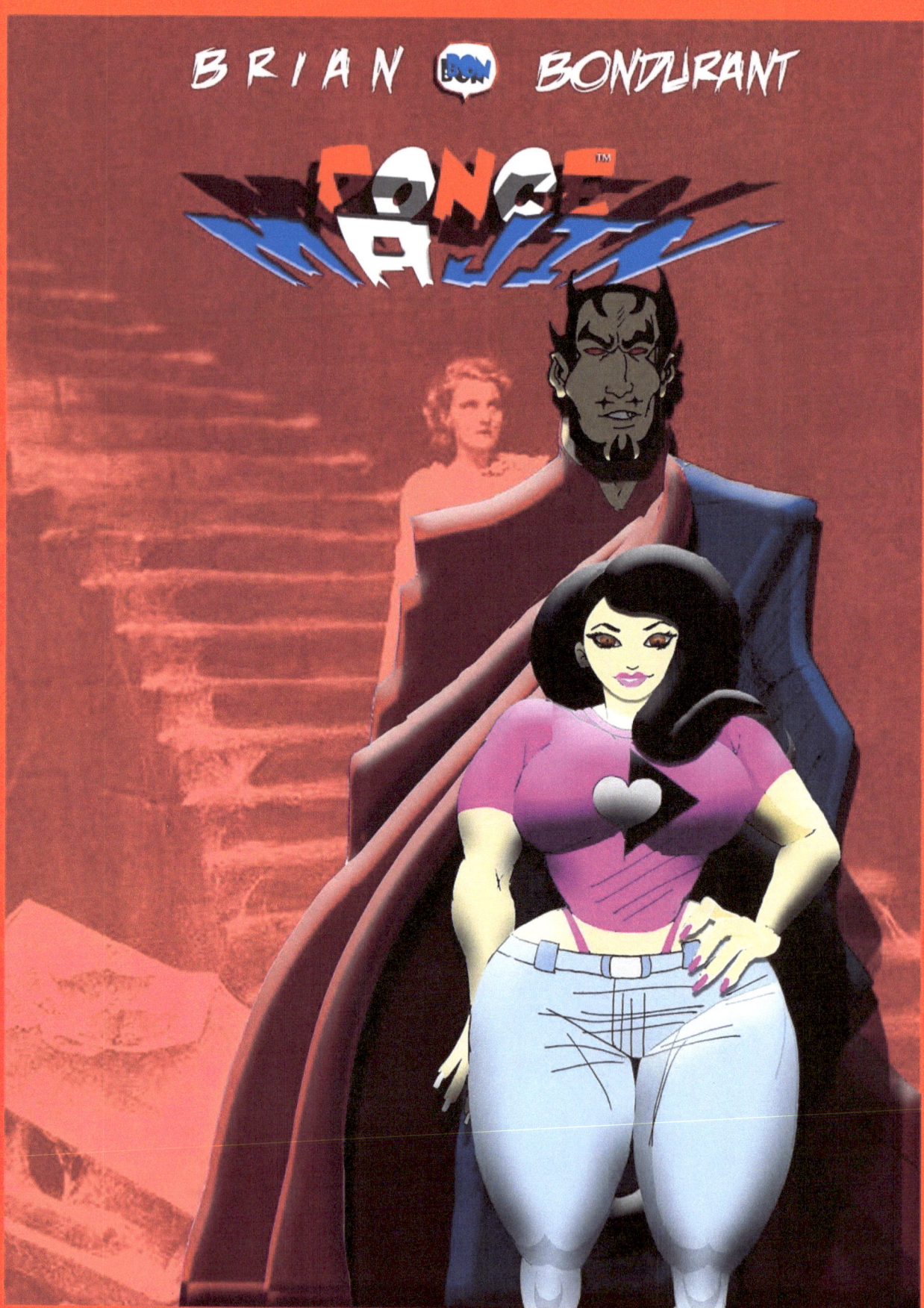

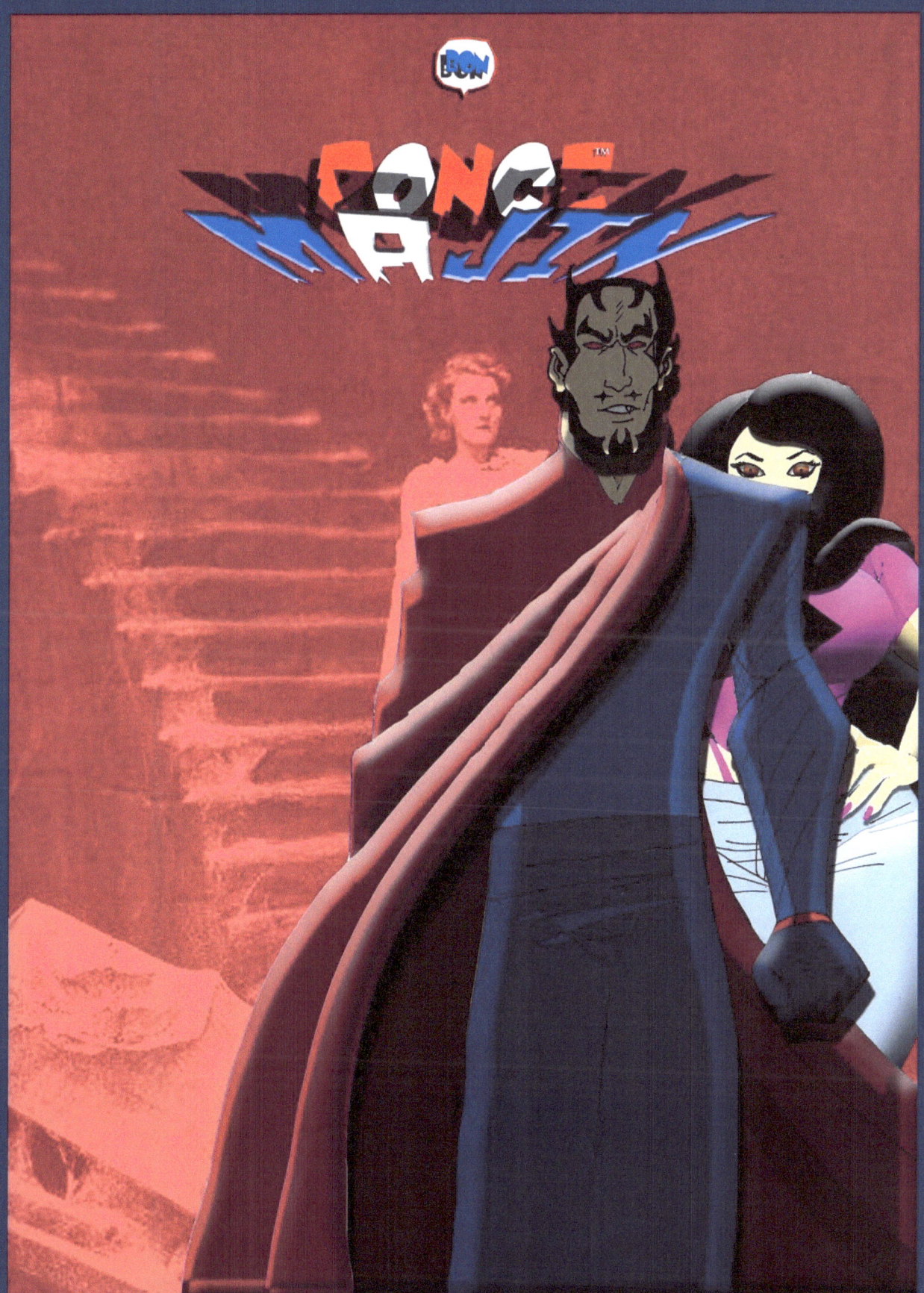

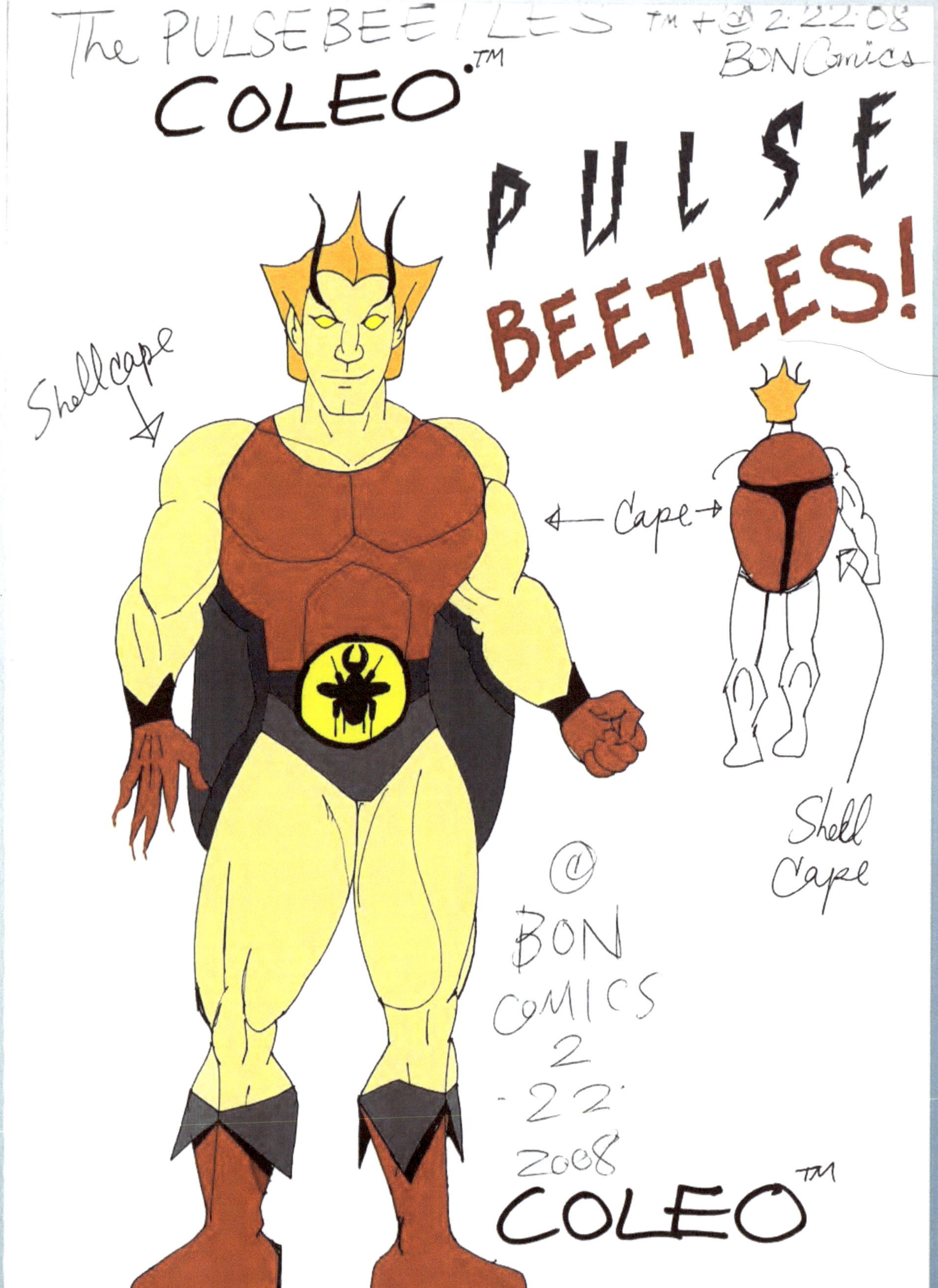
The PULSEBEETLES TM + © 2-22-08
BON Comics
COLEO.TM
PULSE
BEETLES!
Shellcape
Cape
Shell Cape
©
BON
COMICS
2
-22-
2008
COLEO TM

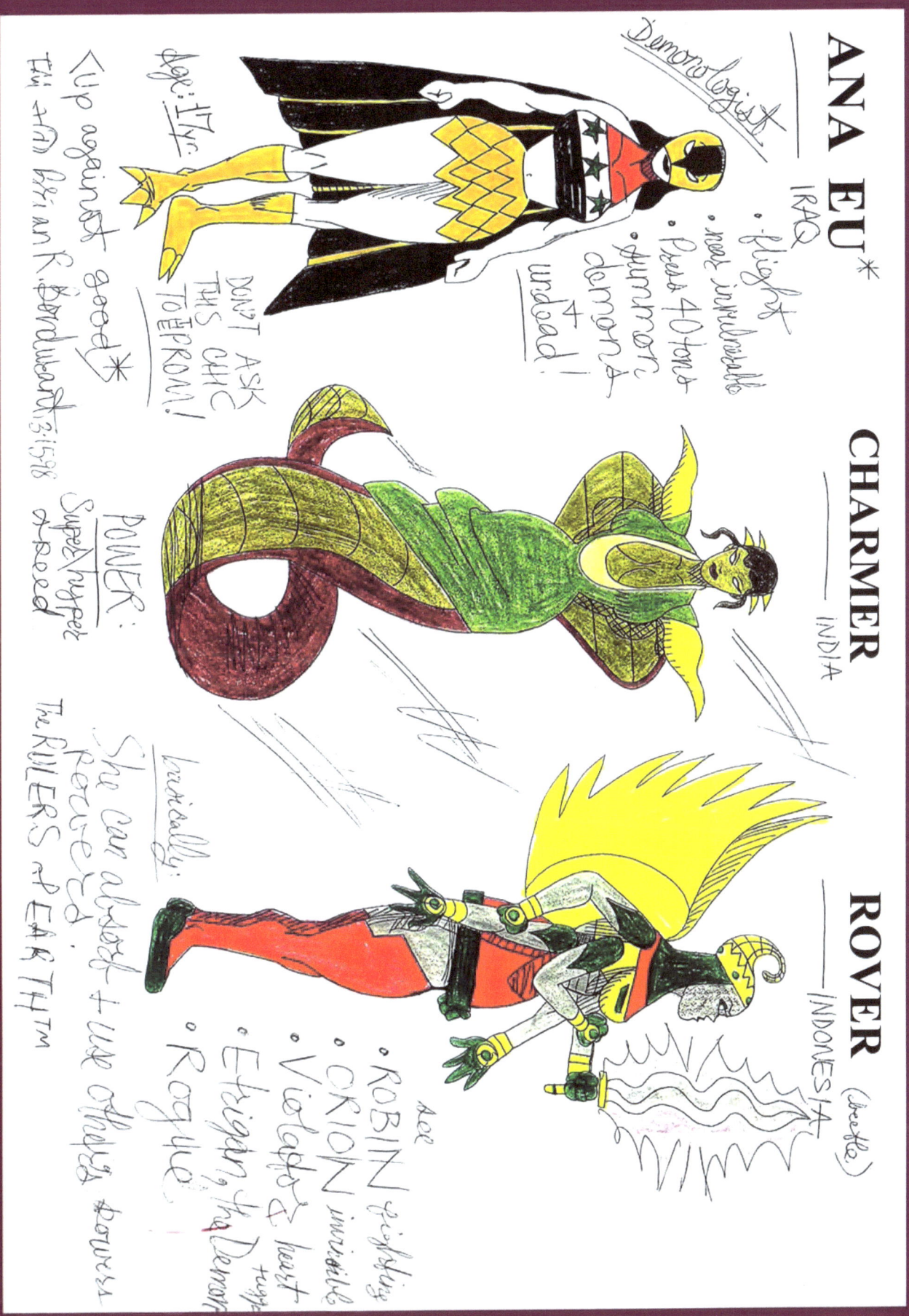

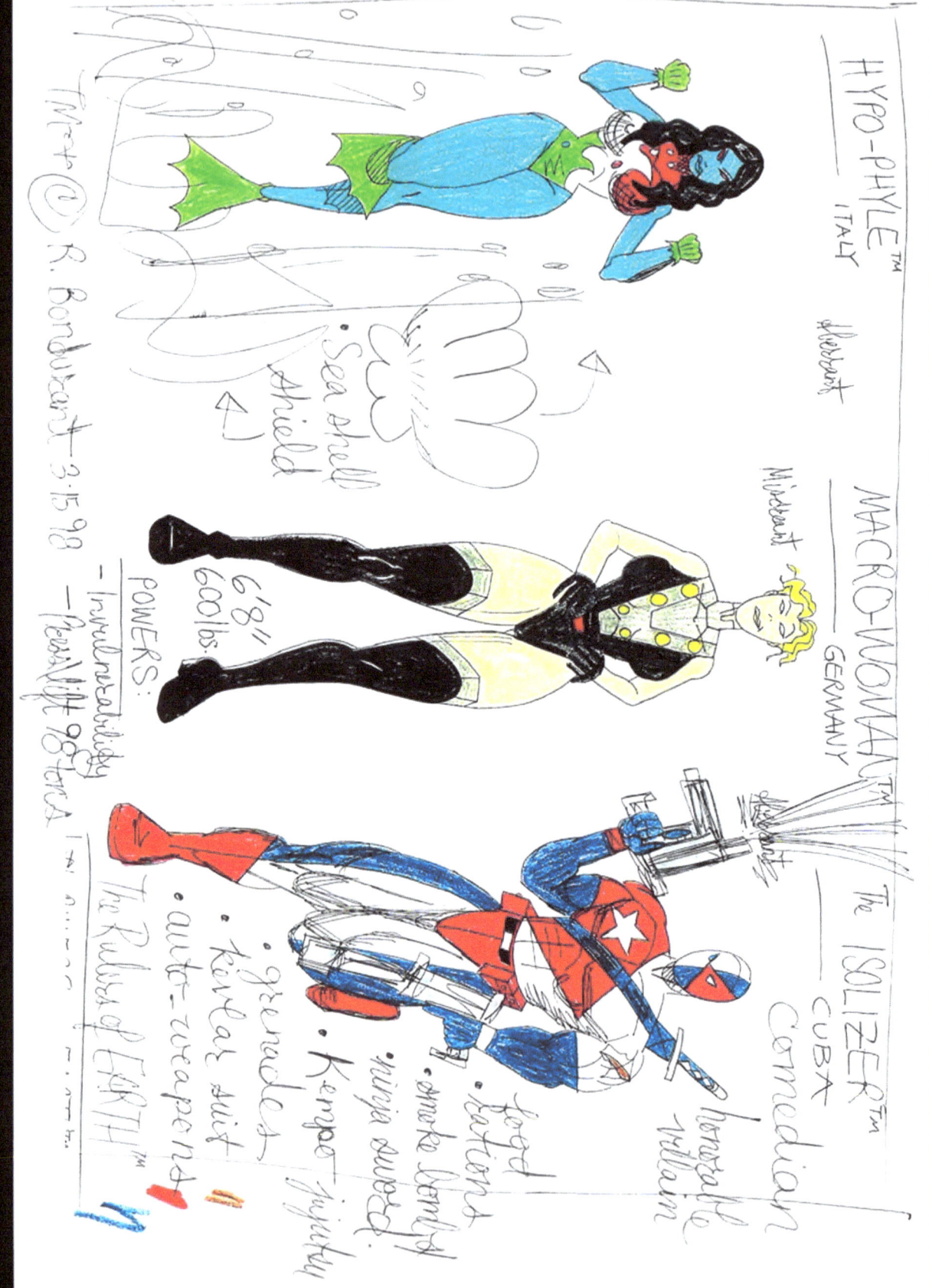

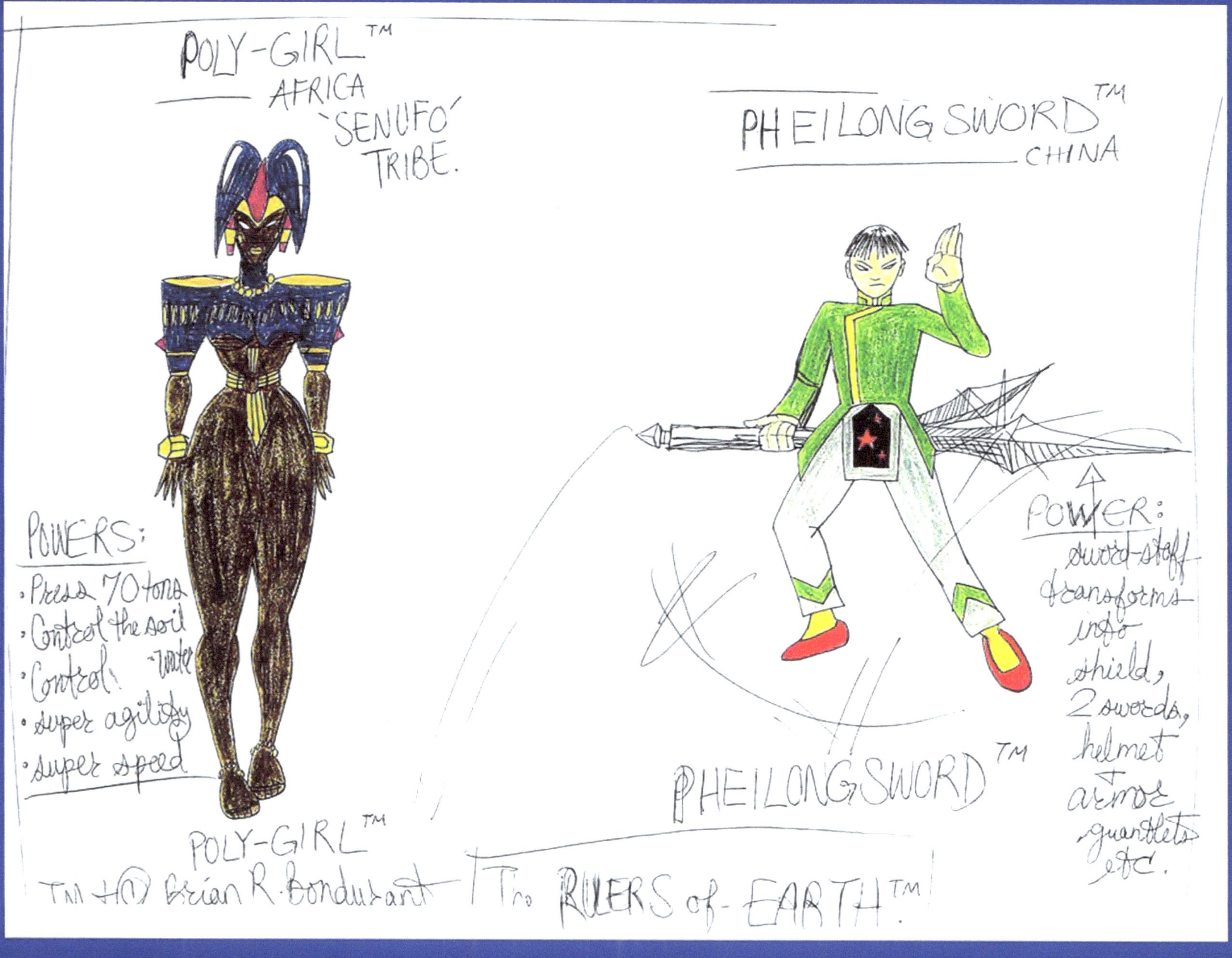

POLY-GIRL ™
AFRICA
"SENUFO"
TRIBE.

PHEI LONG SWORD ™
CHINA

POWER:
- sword-staff transforms into shield,
- 2 swords,
- helmet
- armor
- gauntlets etc.

POWERS:
- Press 70 tons
- Control the soil
- Control water
- super agility
- super speed

PHEI LONG SWORD ™

PHEI LONG SWORD ™

POLY-GIRL ™

TM + © Brian R. Bondurant   The RIVERS of EARTH ™

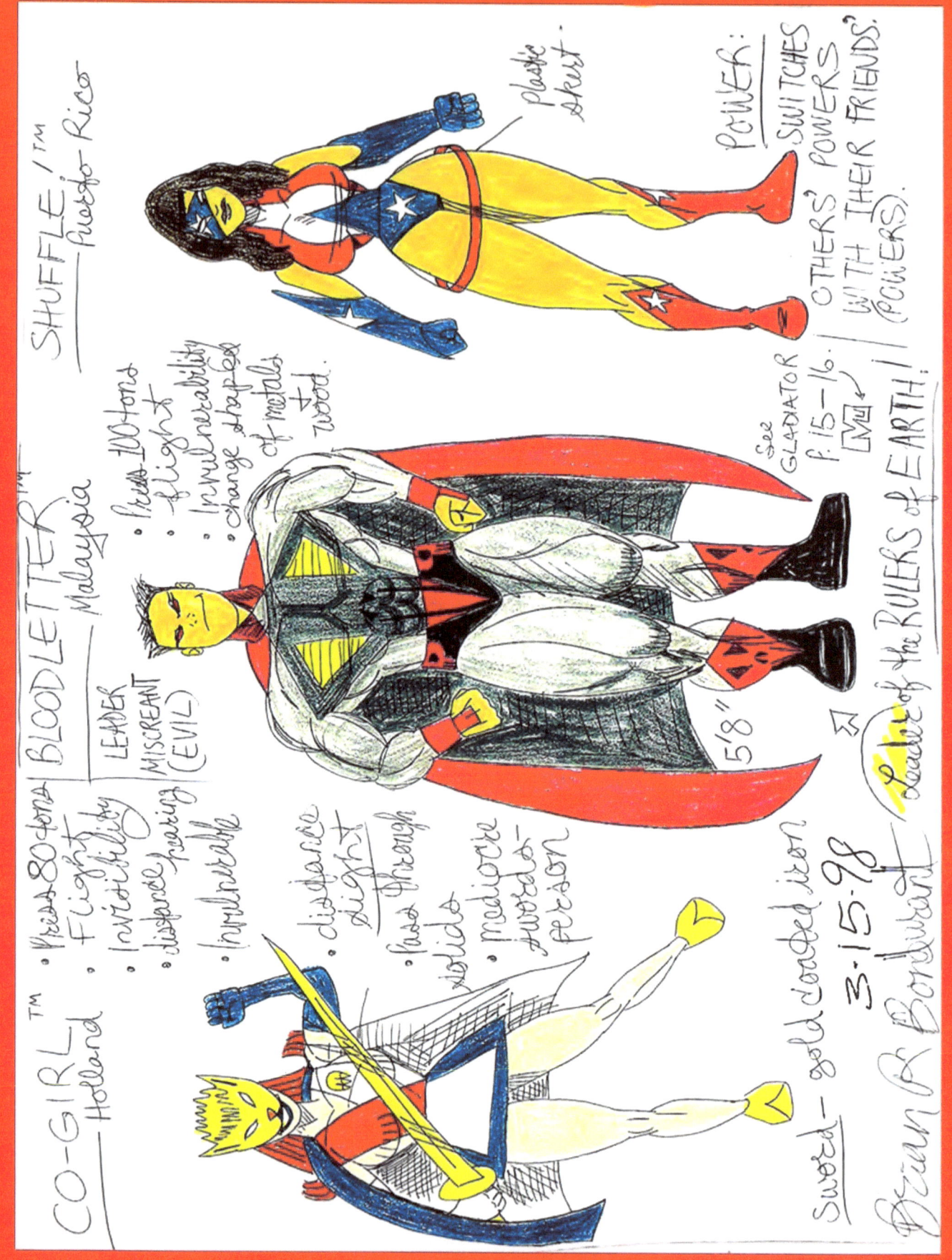

CO-GIRL ™
—Holland

BLOODLETTER ™
—Malaysia

SHUFFLE / ™
—Puerto Rico

LEADER
MISCREANT
(EVIL)

• Press 80 tons
• Flight
• Invisibility
• distance-hearing
• Invulnerable

• Press 100 tons
• Flight
• Invulnerability
• change shapes of metals + wood.

• distance sight
• pass through solids
• mediocre swords-person

plastic skirt.

See GLADIATOR P. 15-16.

POWER:
SWITCHES OTHERS' POWERS WITH THEIR FRIENDS' (POWERS).

Sword — gold-coated iron

3-15-98

Brian A. Bondurant

Leader of the RULERS of EARTH!

5'8"

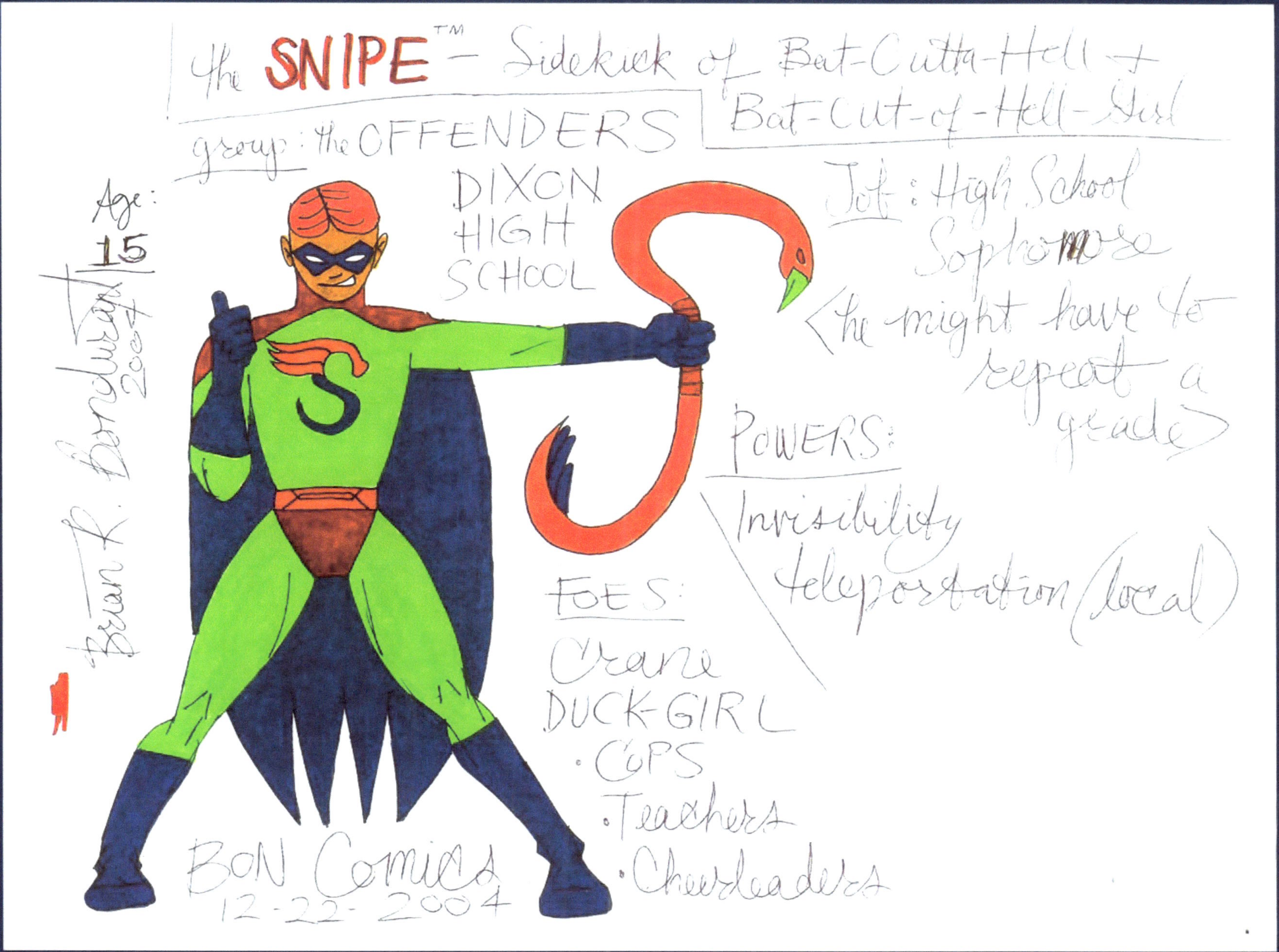
the SNIPE™ - Sidekick of Bat-Outta-Hell + Bat-Out-of-Hell-Girl
group: the OFFENDERS
DIXON HIGH SCHOOL
Job: High School Sophomore
<he might have to repeat a grade>
POWERS:
Invisibility
teleportation (local)
FOES:
Crane
DUCK-GIRL
• COPS
• Teachers
• Cheerleaders
Age: 15
Brian R. Bondurant 2004
BON Comics
12-22-2004

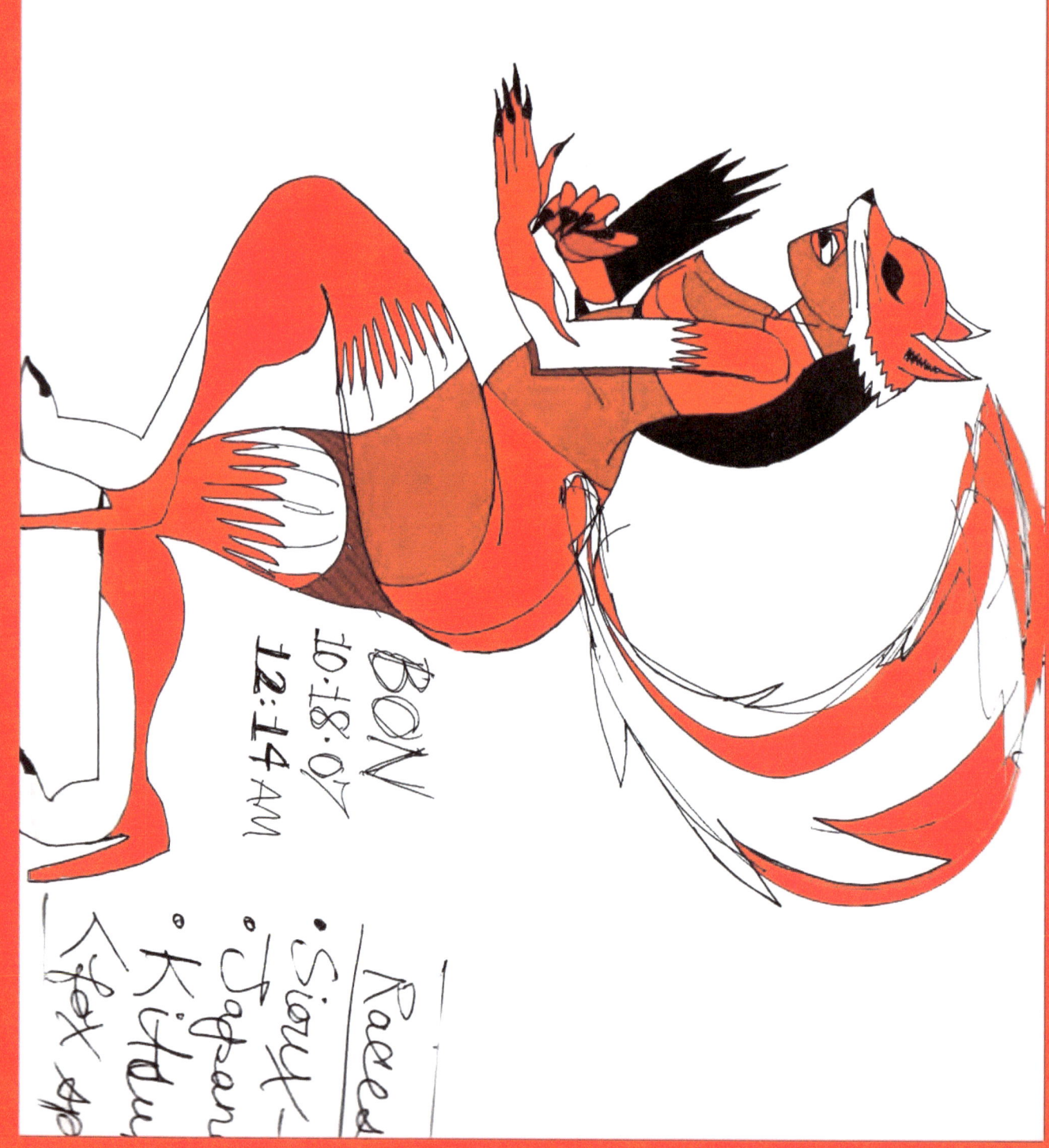

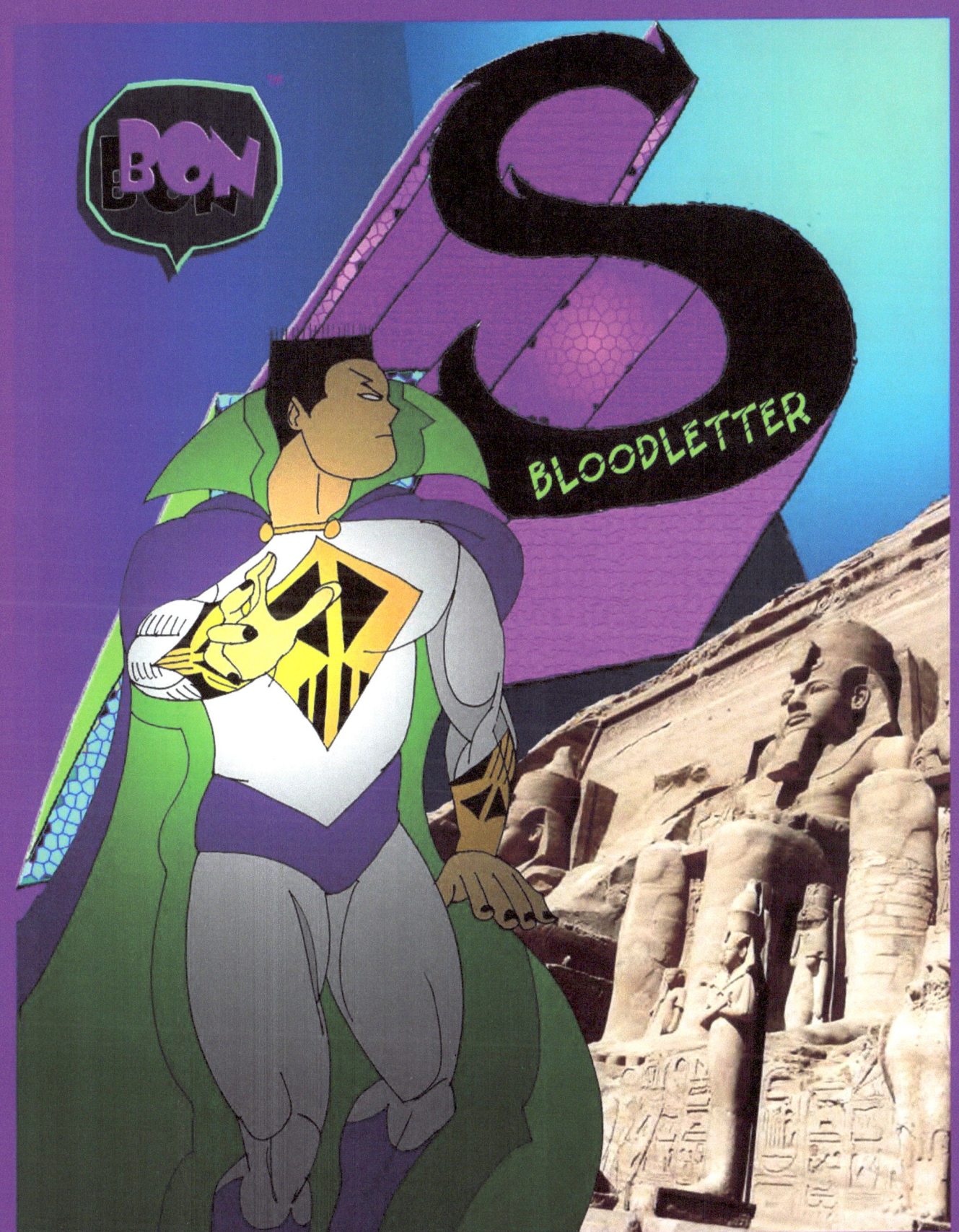

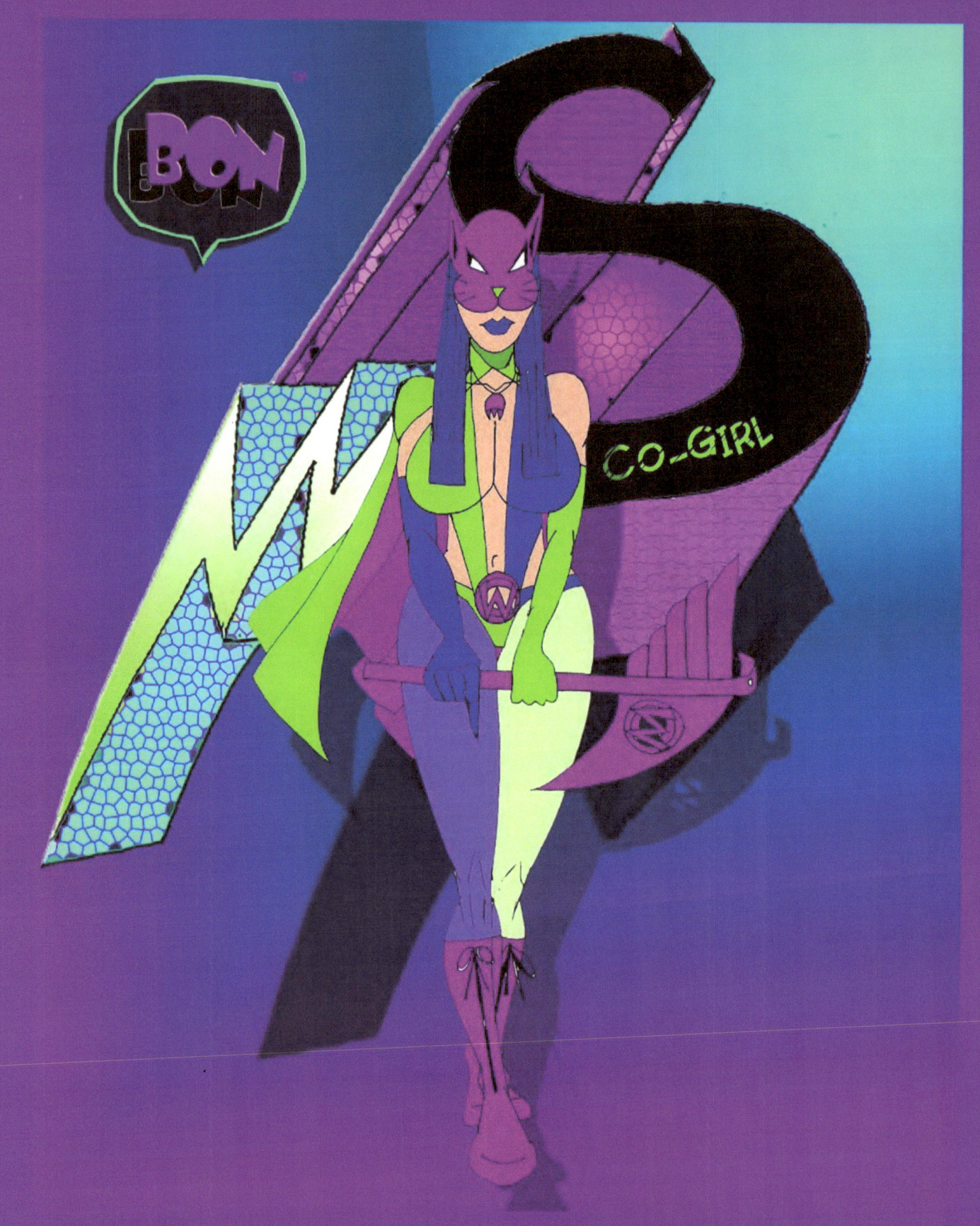

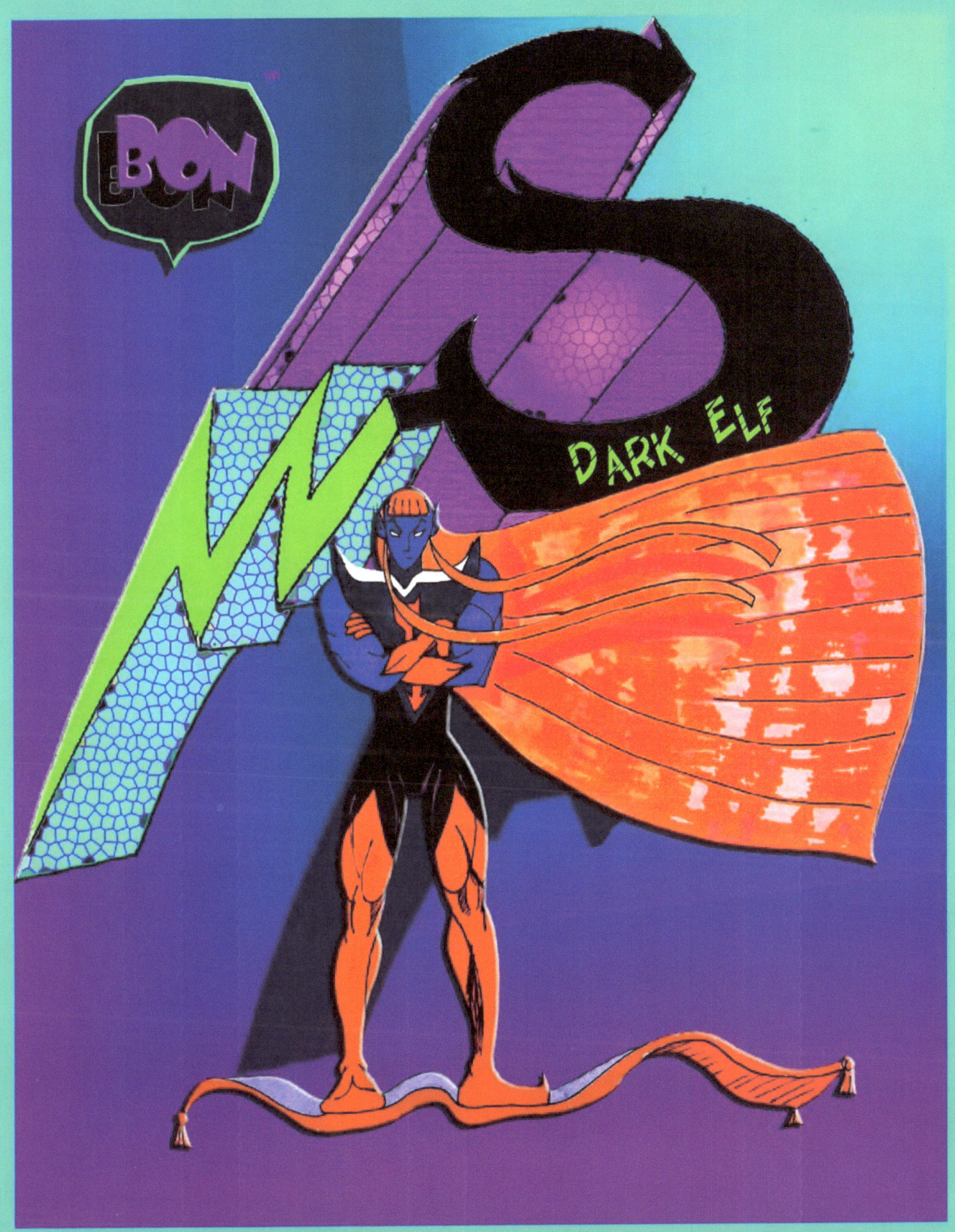

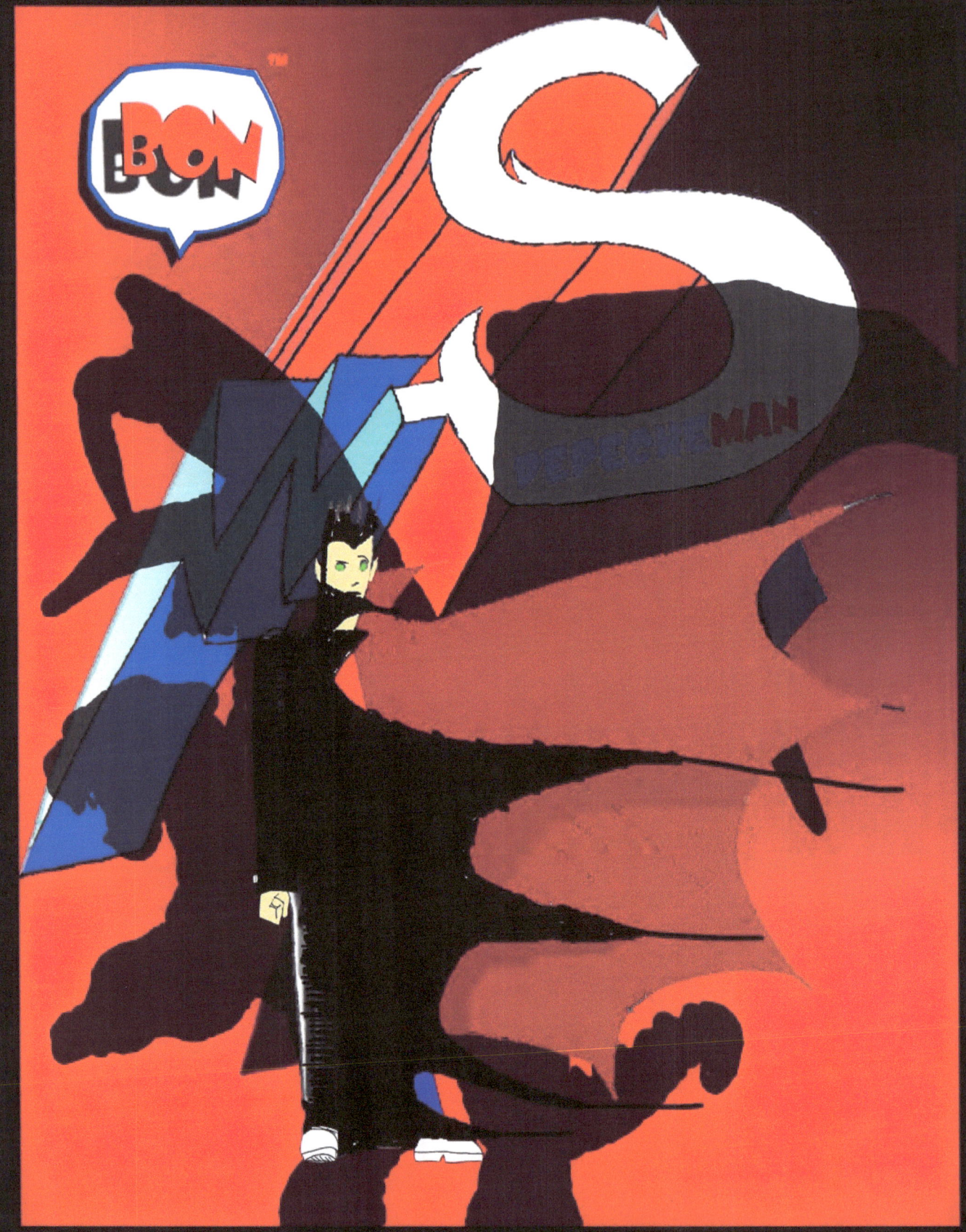

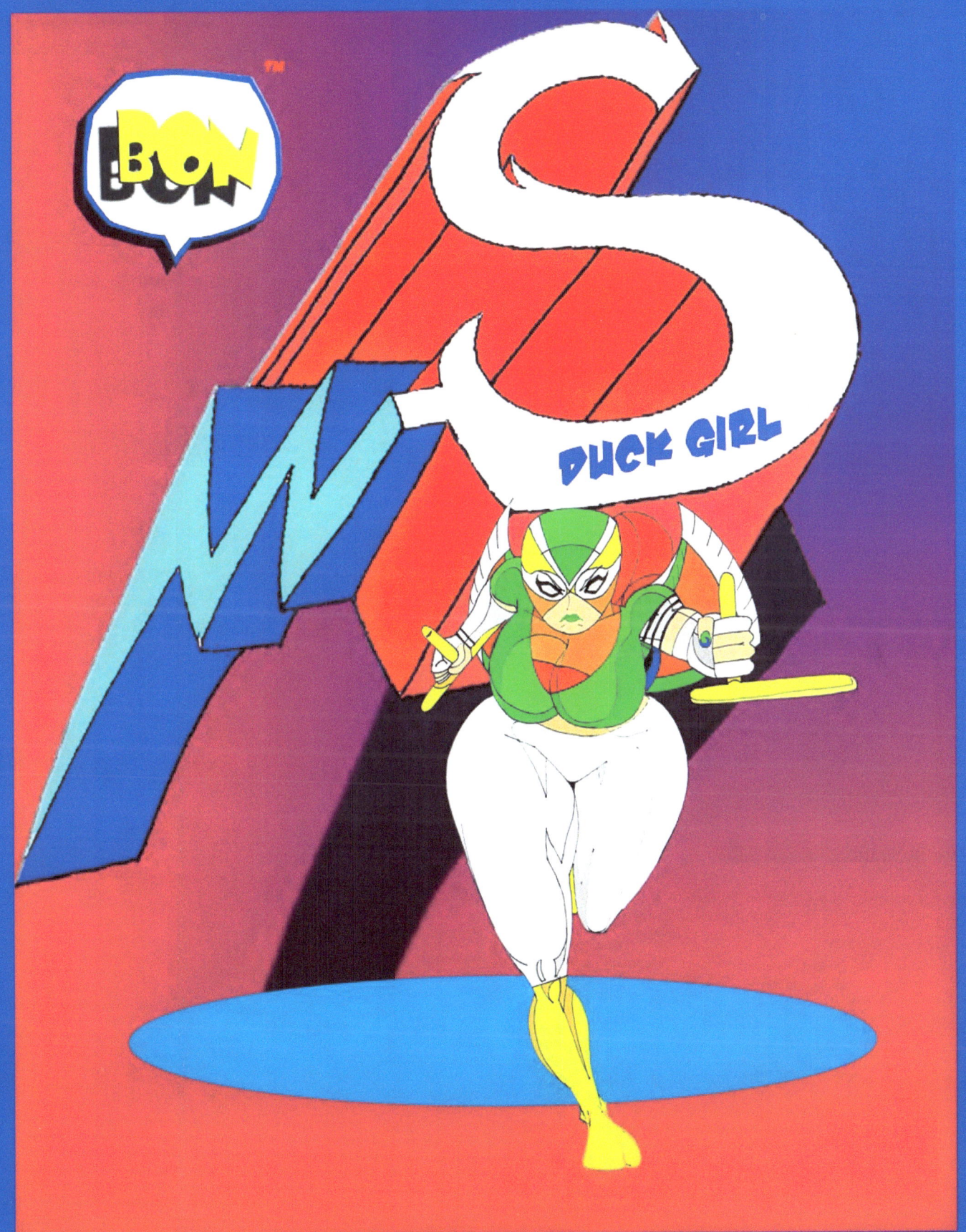

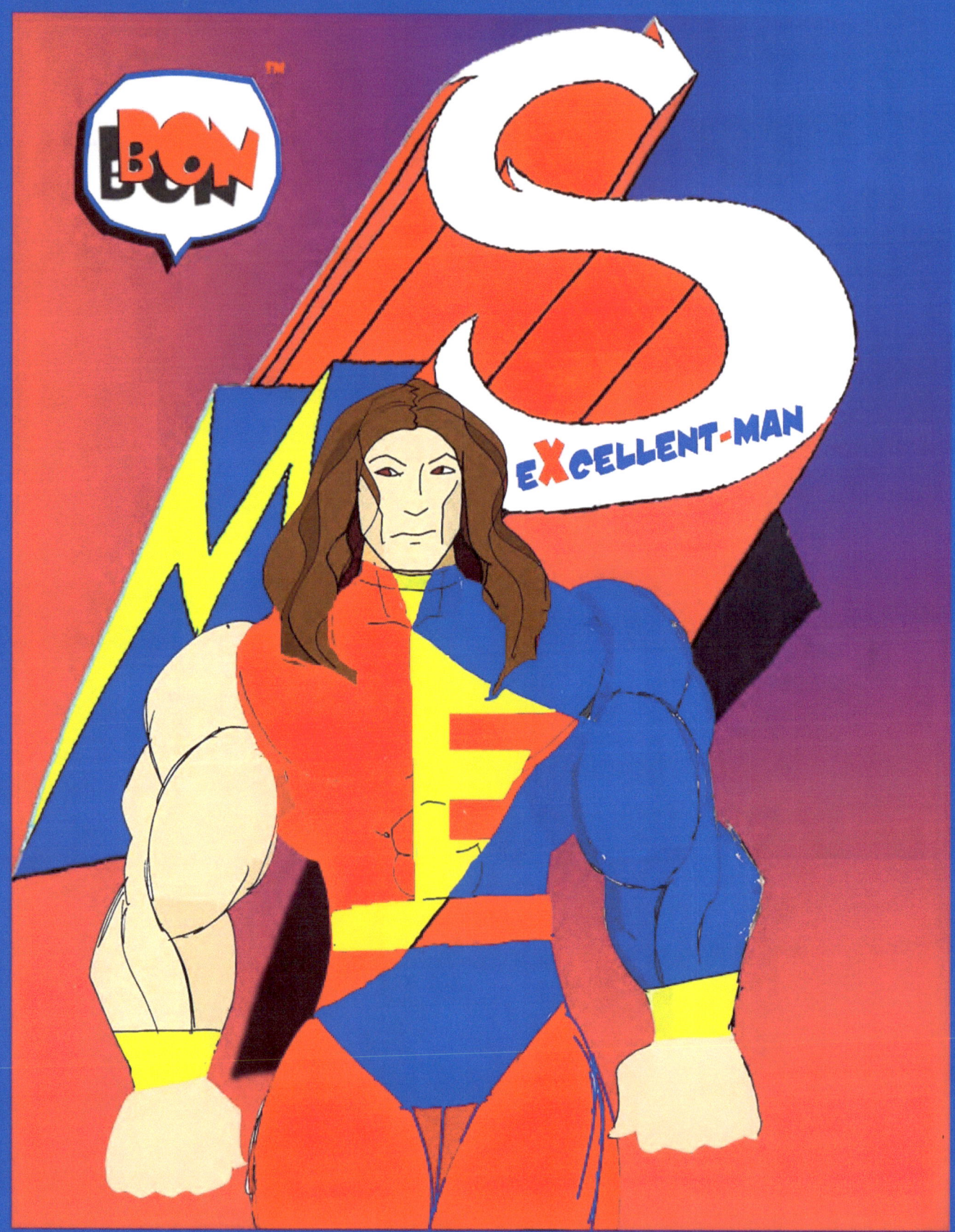

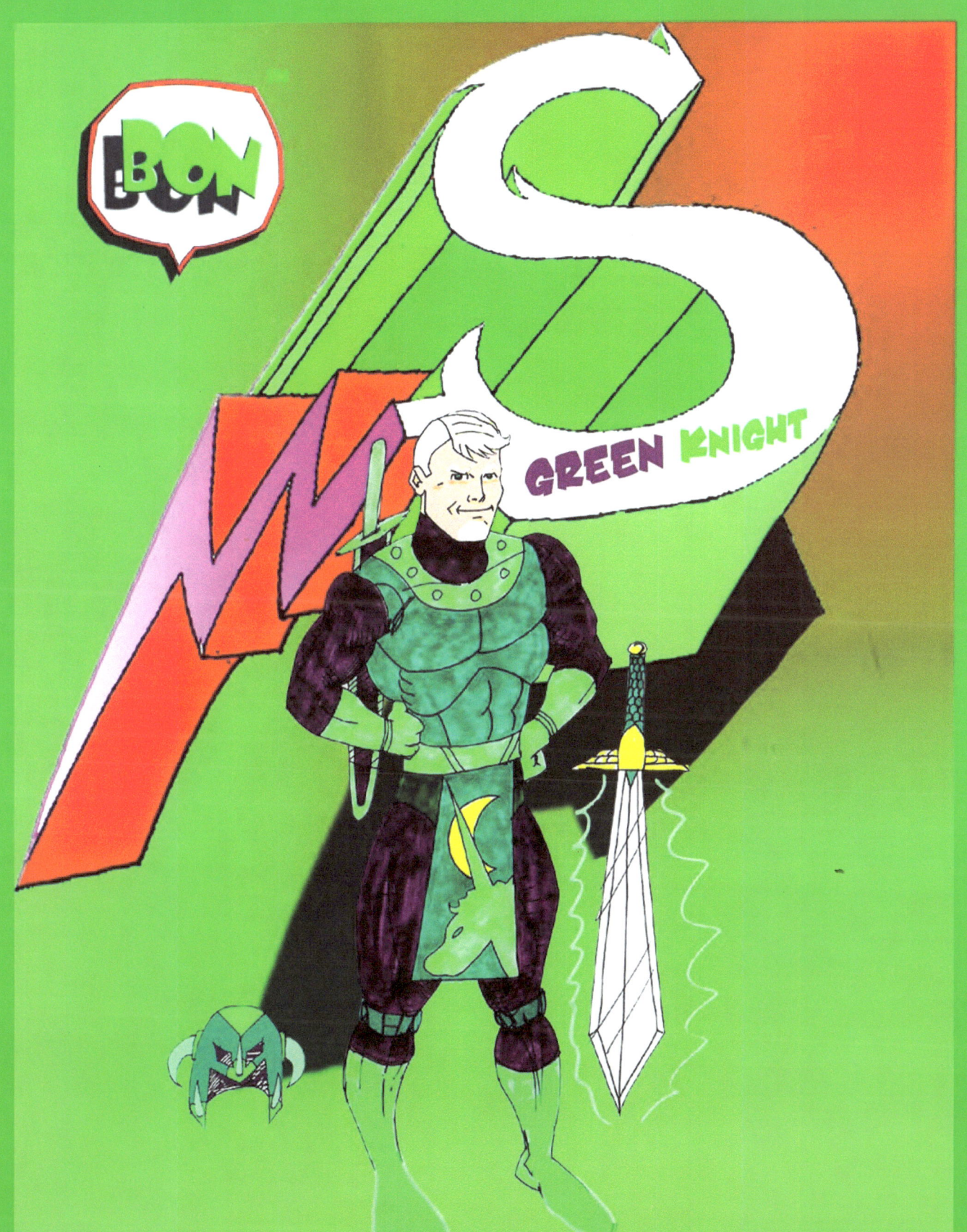

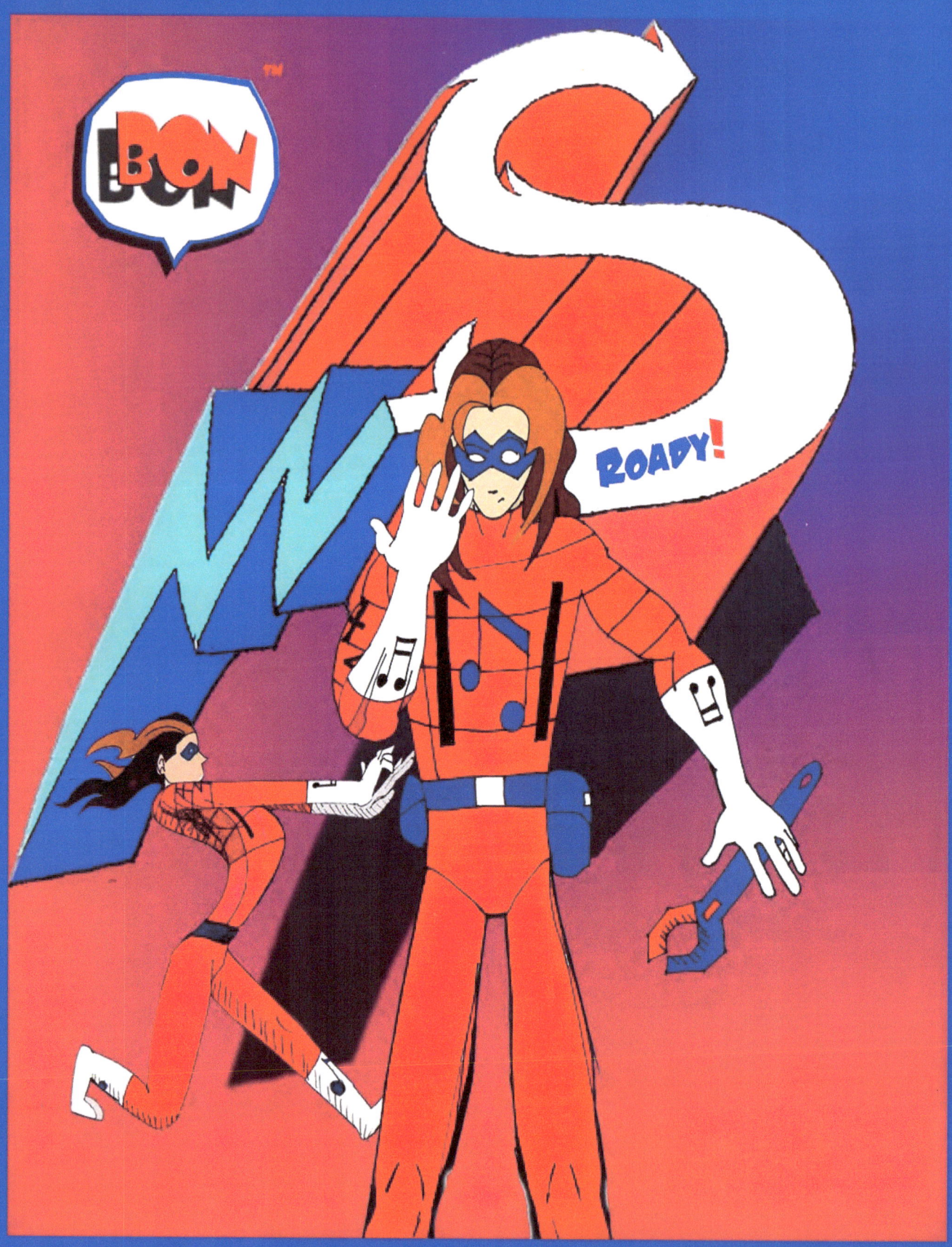

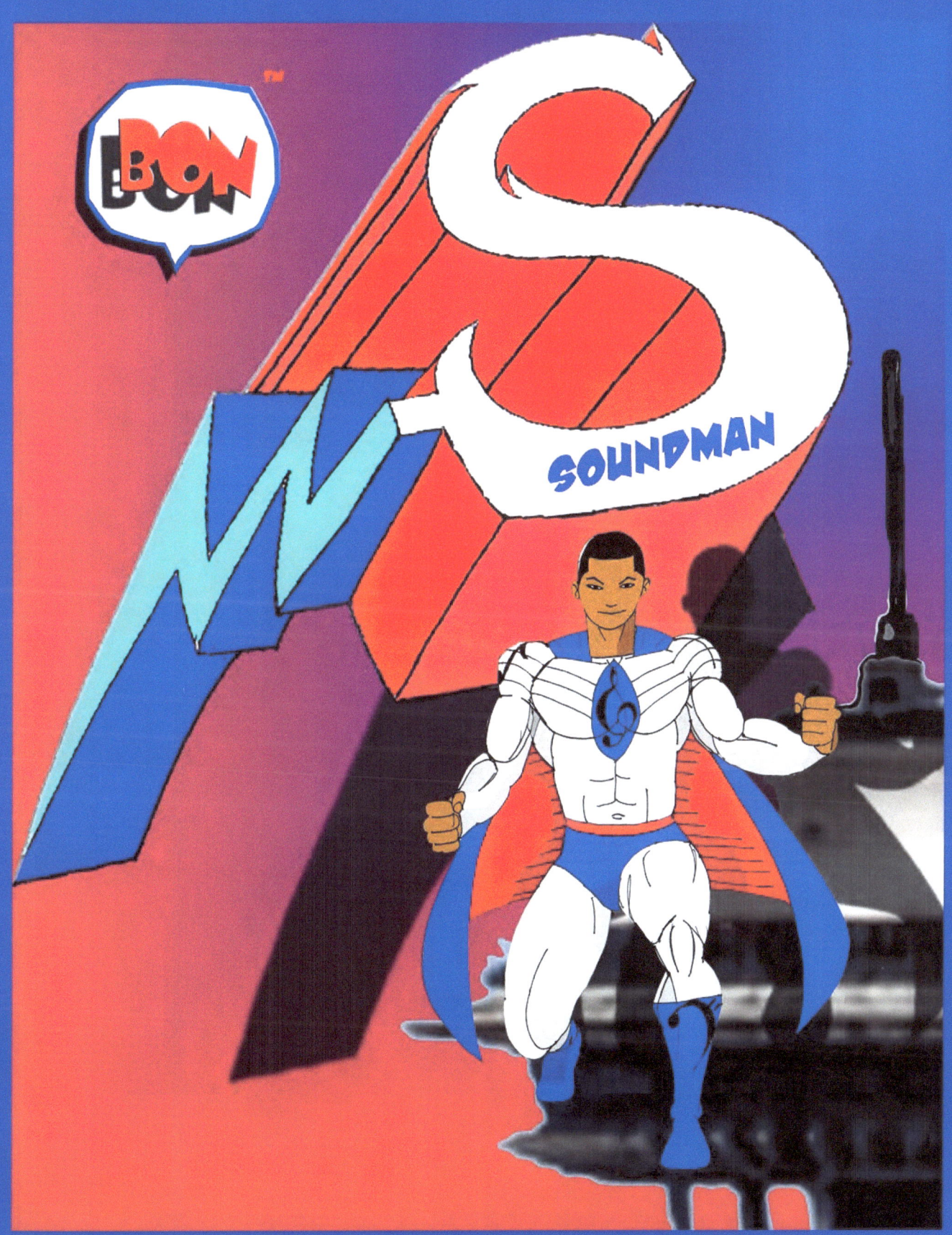

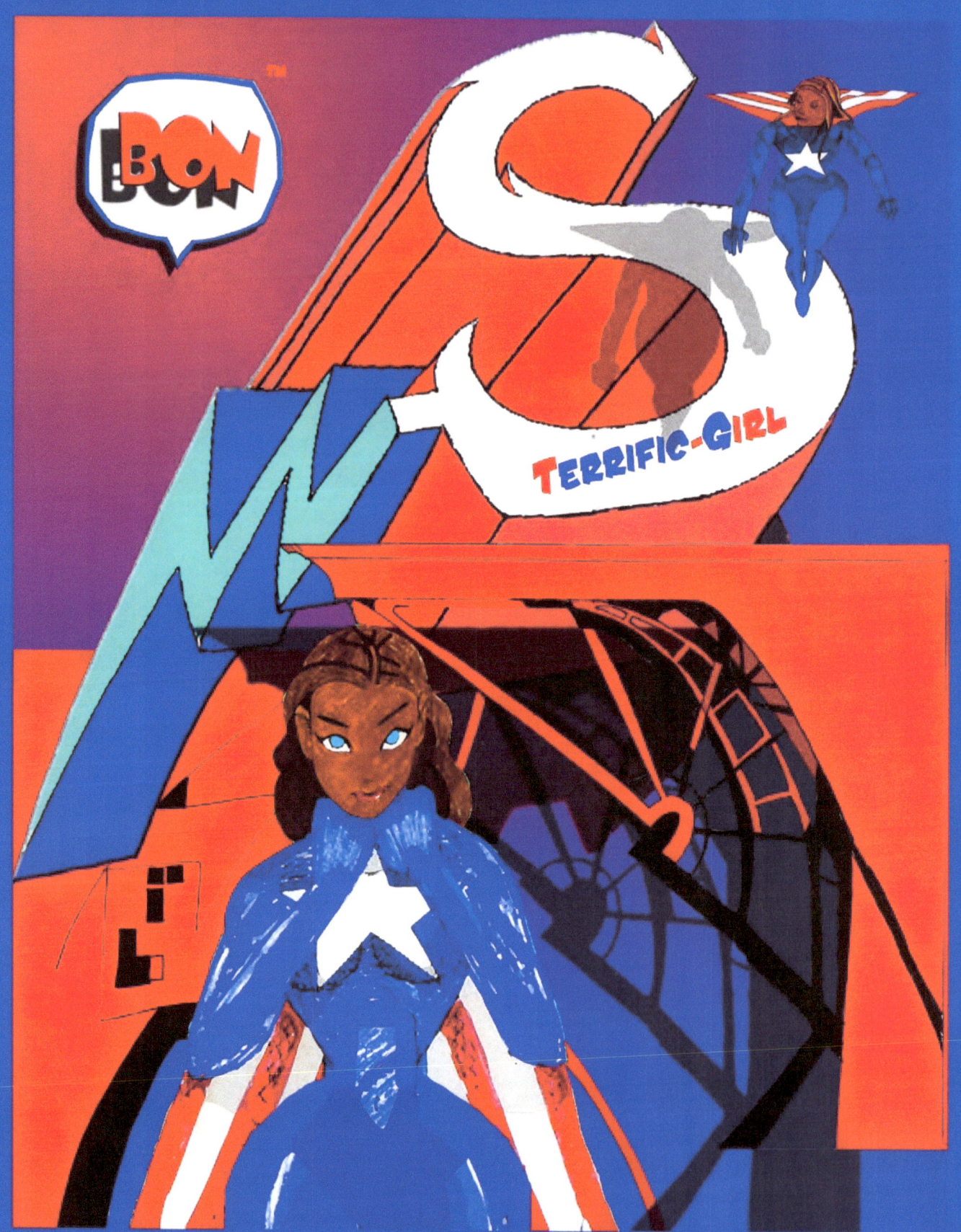

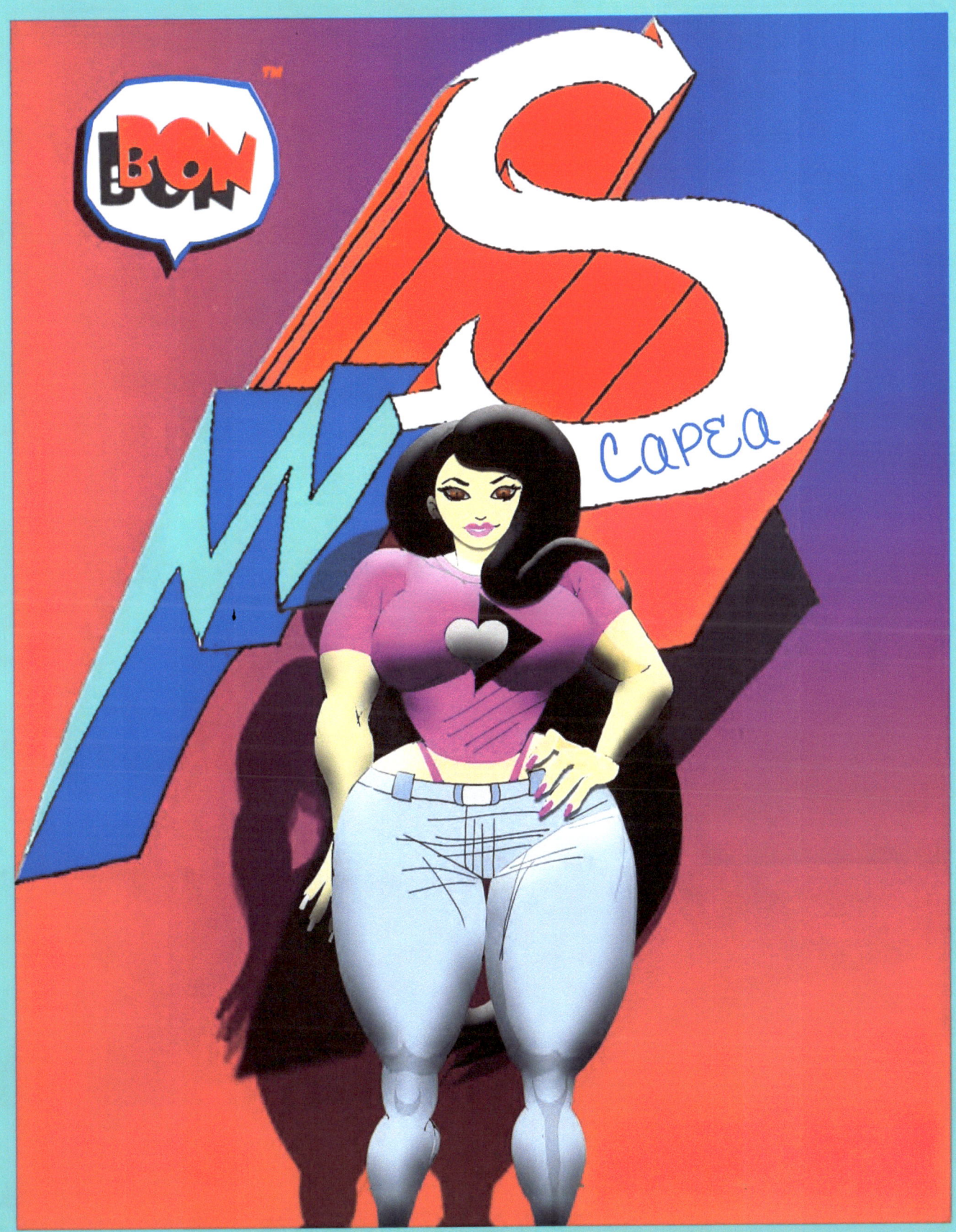

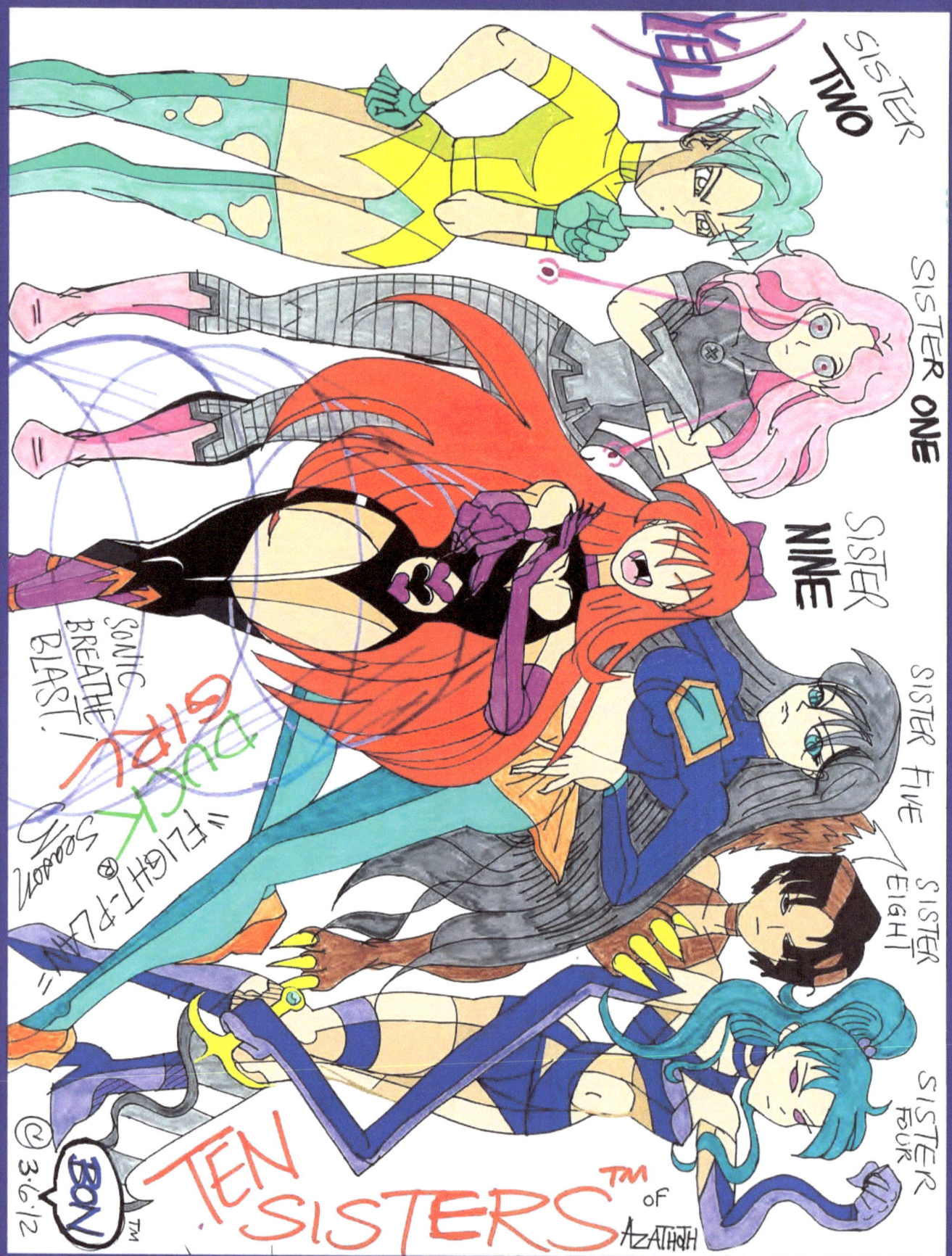

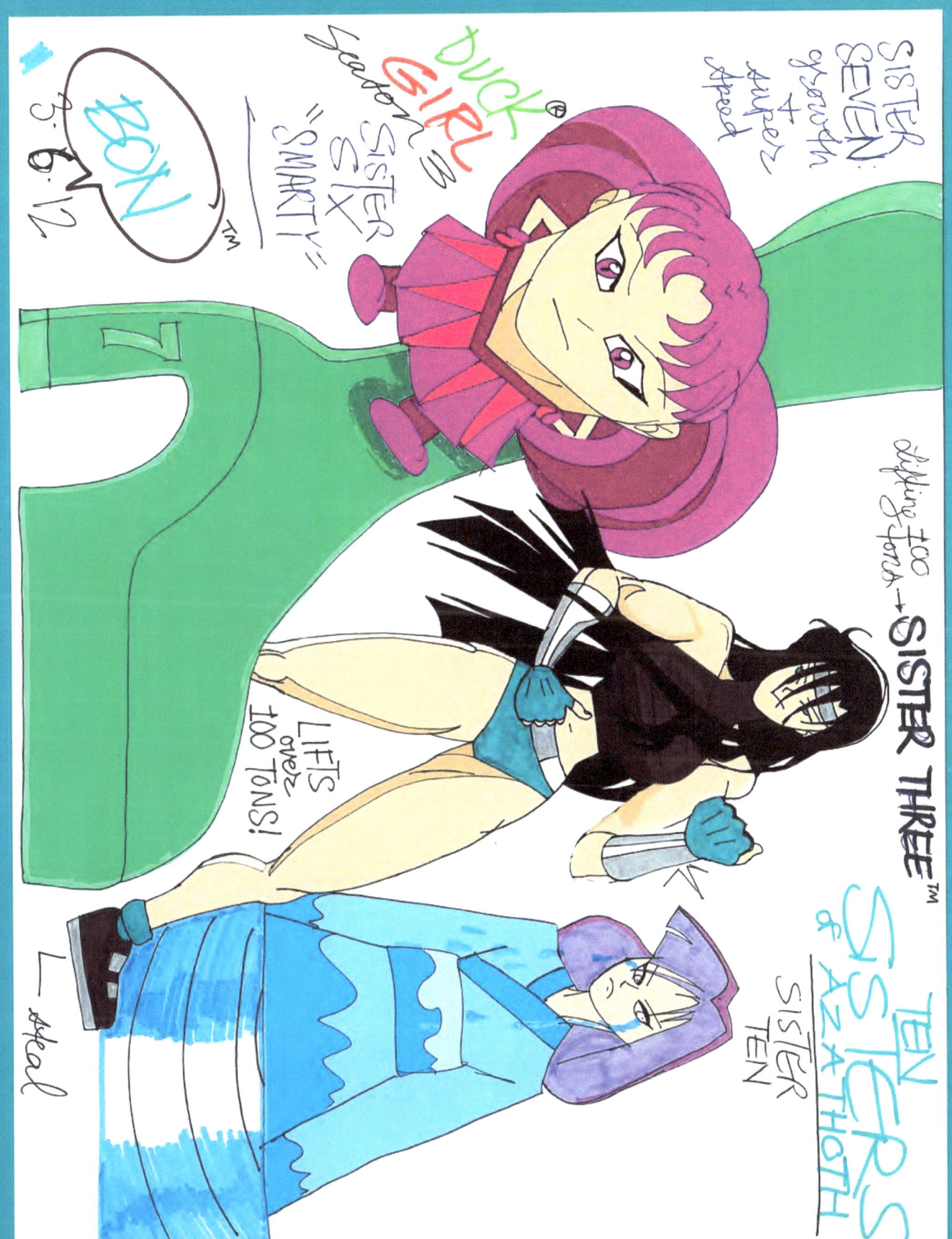

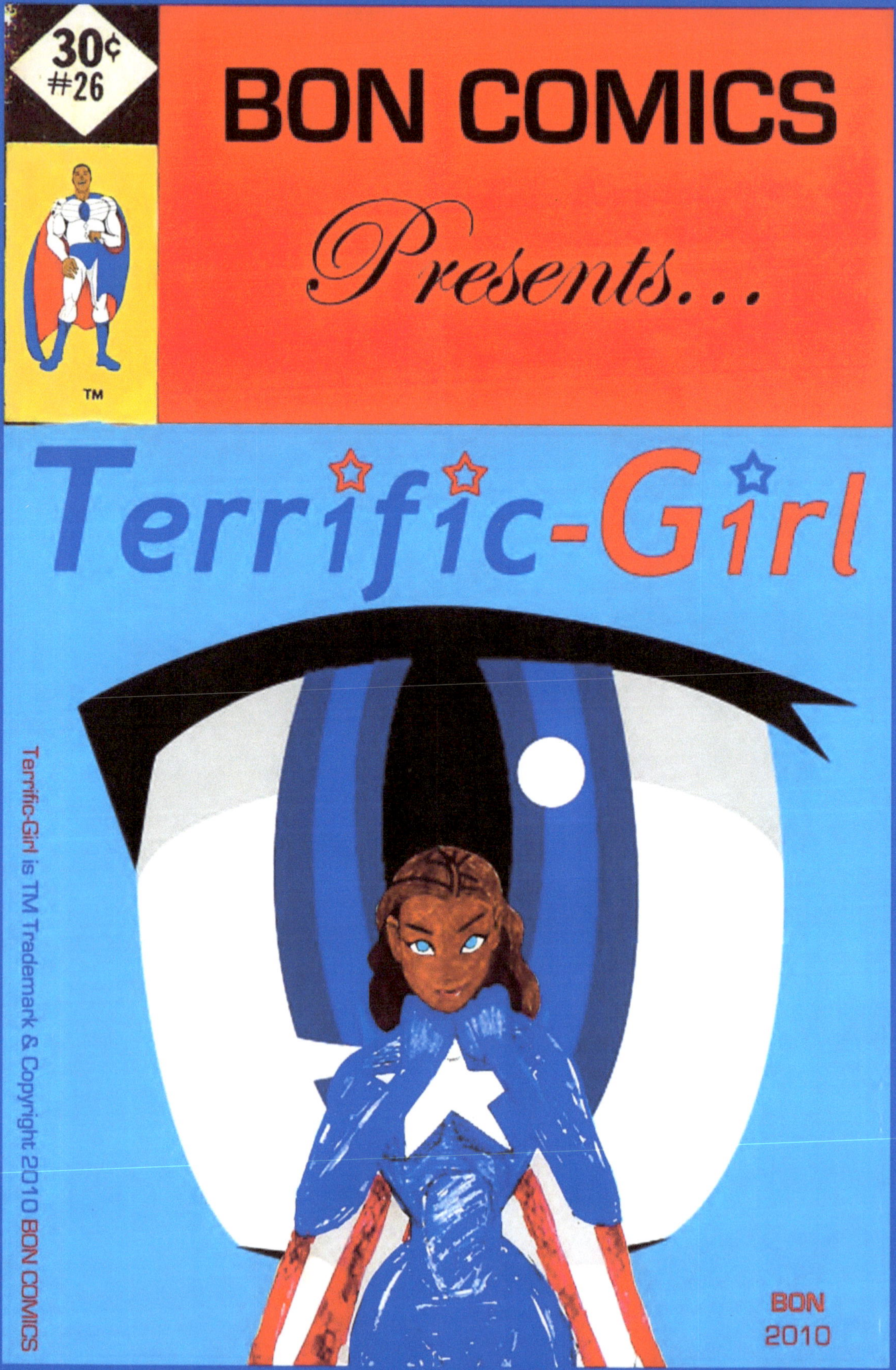

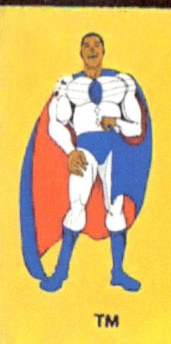

30¢ #26

BON COMICS

Presents...

™

Terrific-Girl

BON 2010

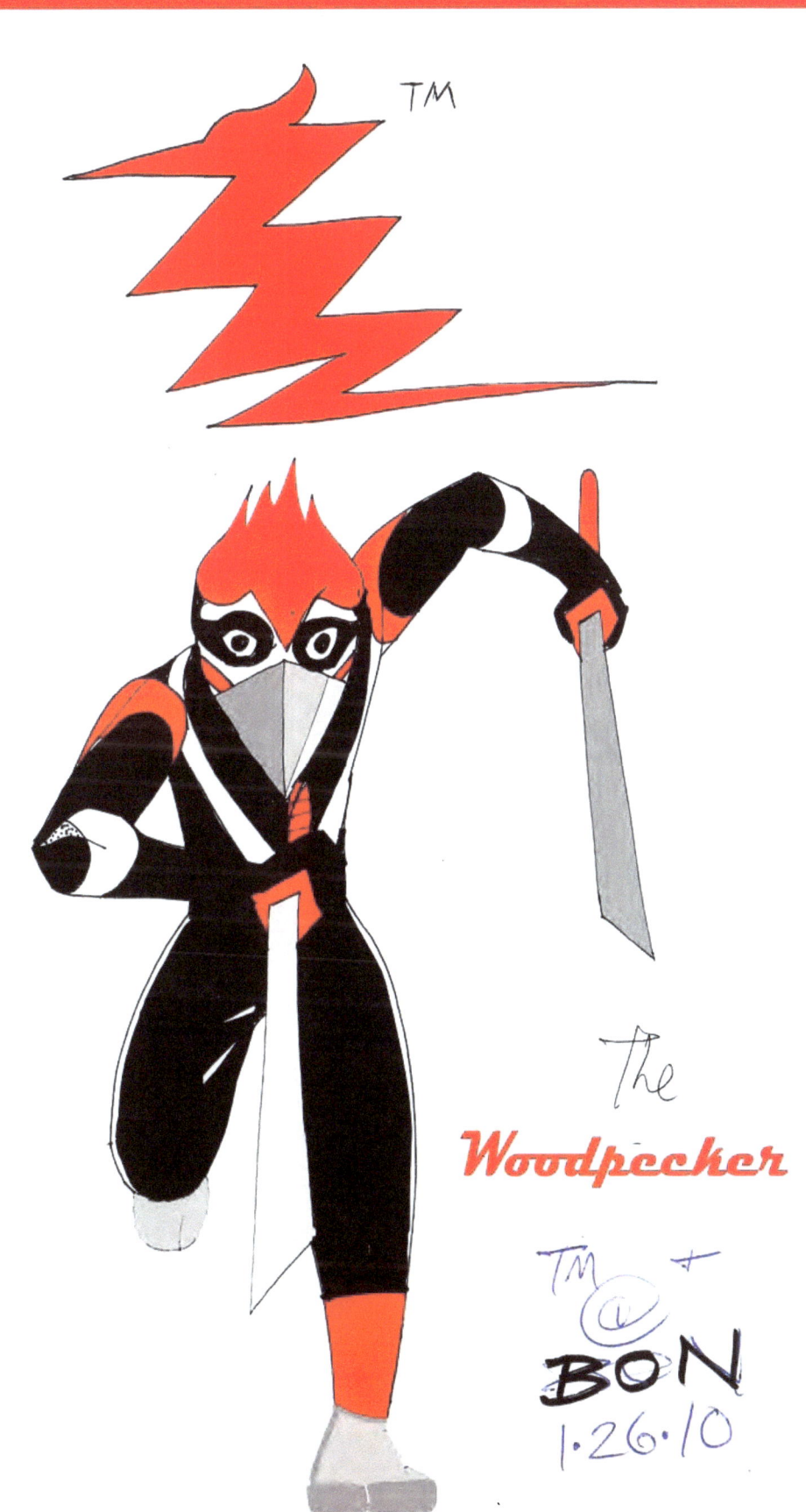

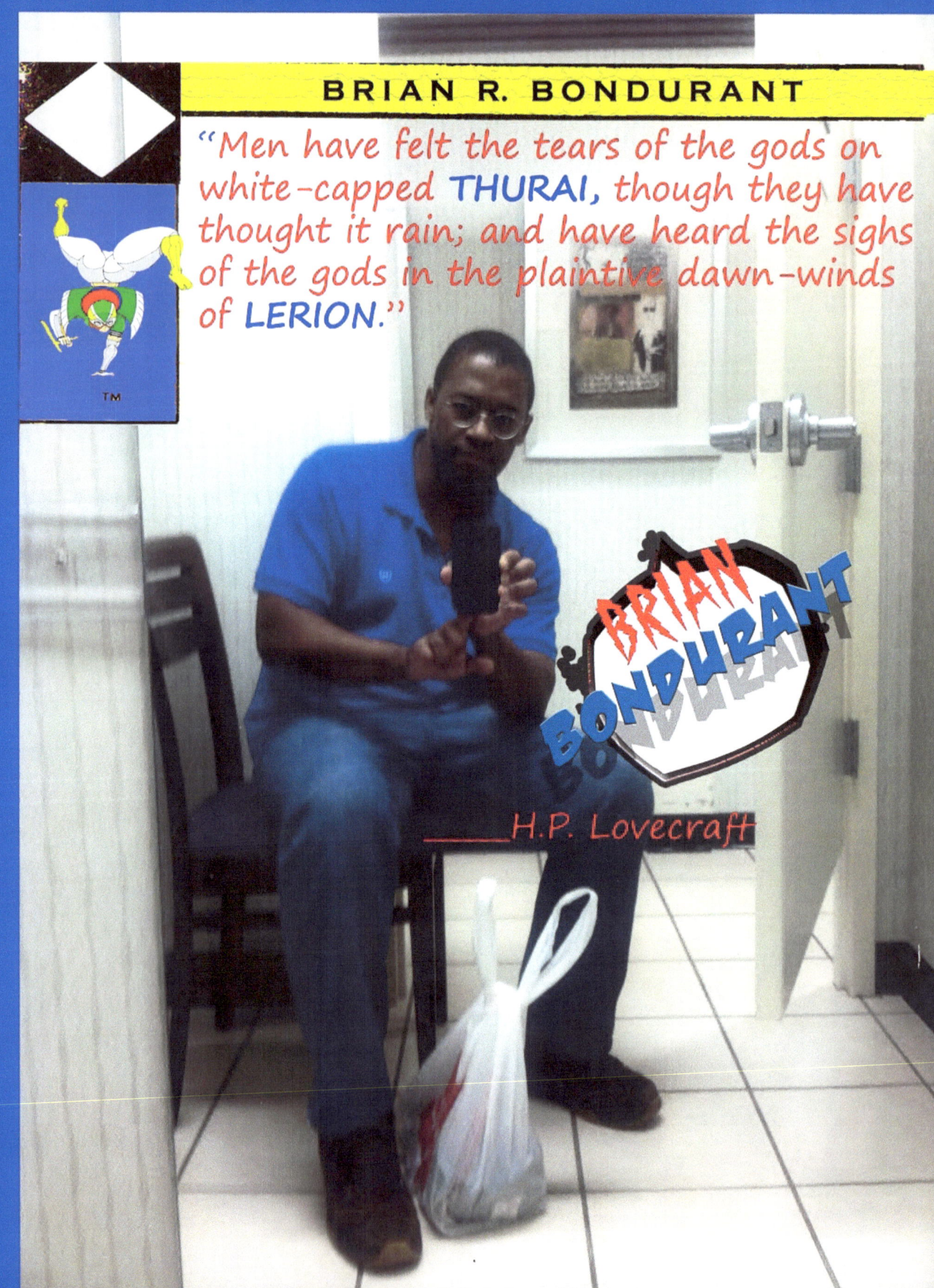

BRIAN R. BONDURANT

"Men have felt the tears of the gods on white-capped **THURAI**, though they have thought it rain; and have heard the sighs of the gods in the plaintive dawn-winds of **LERION**."

—H.P. Lovecraft

www.ingramcontent.com/pod-product-compliance
Lightning Source LLC
Chambersburg PA
CBHW050756180526
45159CB00003B/1477